Wellins Calcott

A candid disquisition of the principles and practices of the Most Ancient and Honourable Society of Free and Accepted Masons

Wellins Calcott

A candid disquisition of the principles and practices of the Most Ancient and Honourable Society of Free and Accepted Masons

ISBN/EAN: 9783337196646

Printed in Europe, USA, Canada, Australia, Japan

Cover: Foto ©Andreas Hilbeck / pixelio.de

More available books at **www.hansebooks.com**

[illegible]ID DISQUISITI[illegible]

OF THE

[illegible]NCIPLES and PRACTICES

OF THE MOST

Ancient and Honourable SOCIETY of

Free and Accepted Masons;

TOGETHER WITH

Some STRICTURES on the ORIGIN, NATURE, and DESIGN of that INSTITUTION.

DEDICATED, BY PERMISSION,

To the most Noble and most Worshipful
HENRY DUKE *of* BEAUFORT, &c. &c.
GRAND MASTER.

By WELLINS CALCOTT, *P. M.*

—— —— Ab ipso
Ducit opes animumque ferro.

HOR. OD.

LONDON:
Printed for the AUTHOR,
By Brother JAMES DIXWELL, in *St. Martin's Lane.*
A. L. 5769. A. D. 1769.

And while they endear your Grace to every humane heart, must also inspire the friends to our *society*, with the most lively sentiments of gratitude and pleasure, both for your Grace's attention, and known goodness to particular brethren, and your readiness to propose and adopt every measure, calculated to add dignity to our establishment, and give energy and authority to its laws.

This glorious prospect gives us the fullest hopes, that under your Grace's illustrious patronage, the benign sentiments of charity, and the indispensible duty of promoting the general welfare of mankind, will be more universally and extensively received.

Encouraged by these considerations, I flatter myself, your Grace will forgive my endeavour to secure permanency to the following sheets, by prefixing a name, which must be revered by every friend to the interest of humanity, and the benevolent intentions of our institution, till time and masonry shall be no more.

May it please your GRACE,

Your GRACE's most dutiful,

And devoted humble servant,

A LIST OF SUBSCRIBERS NAMES.

The Most Noble and Most Worshipful *Henry, Duke of Beaufort,* &c. &c. G. M.

The Hon. *Charles Dillon,* W. D. G. M.

Rowland Holt, Esq; W. S. G. W.

Mr. *John Jaffray,* W. J. G. W.

Rowland Berkley, Esq; G. T.

Mr. *Thomas French,* G. S.

A

MR Henry Adams, Attorney at Law, S. to the Cornubian Lodge, at Launceston, Cornwall
Mr. H. Adean, Long Acre
Mr. J. Adams, Mariner
Mr. Adams of Torwood, Devon.
Mr. Robert Adamson, Page of the back Stairs to his Royal Highness the Duke of Gloucester
Mr. Parmenas Adcock, Tower-hill
Mr. Seth Agar, York
Mr. Samuel Akerman, Grocer, Bristol
Mr. Thomas Alker, Lawford's Gate, Bristol

William Allen, Esq; St. James's, Roy. P
Mr. William Allen, of the Plymouth D
W. S. W.
Mr. Thomas Allard, Taylor, Bristol, P
Mr. Allanson, Mercer, St. Clement's C
Rev. Mr. Allen, Helston, Cornwall
Thomas Alleyne, Esq; Bennet Street, W
Mr. Allison, Printer, Falmouth, P. M.
Mr. William Anderton, Surgeon, at Ba
Mr. Edward Anderson, Chelsea
Mr. Burt. Anderson, Ditto
Mr. Ansell, Linen Draper, Bath
Mr. Anthony, Mercer, St. Ives, Cornw
Mr. George Antrobus, Clog-maker, Bri
Mr. Andrews, Distiller, Craven's Buil
Mr. Arno, of Arno's Vale, near Bristol
Mr. Ashley, the Talbot Inn, Strand, R.
Mr. Ashley, Purser in the Royal Navy,
Mr. William Ash, ditto
Mr. J. Ashfield, the King's Arms Lodge,
Mr. William Askwith, Ripon, Yorkshire
Mr. H. Atwood, Surgeon, Bath, P. M.
Mr. T. W. Atwood, of ditto
Mr. R. Atwood, of ditto, S.
Mr. Atkinson, Apothecary, Pallmall, R
John Aubrey, Esq; Member of Parliame
William Aveline, Esq; Oxford Road
Mr. Benjamine Axford, Brazier, Stall St
Lieutenant Richard Aylmer, 17th Regi
Ilminster

B

His Grace the Duke of Buccleugh, R. P.
Right Hon. Lord Viscount Bateman, R. P
The Hon. Arthur Barry, Cheshire
John Harris Barrington, Esq; Radnorshir
Mr. James Bayley, Bristol
Mr. James Barr, ditto
Mr. William Ball, S. St. George's Lo.
Mr. Ralph Banks, of Crœmill Passage,
Mr. Thomas Batty, Plymouth Dock
Mr. J. Bayley, Attorney at Law, ditto
Mr. M. Bailey, Half Moon Tavern, Sal
Mr. Robert Barron, Brazier, Plymouth
Mr. Robert Bailey, Taylor, ditto
Capt. John Barclay of the Marines, ditto
Mr. John Badcock of Penzance

Mr. Andrew Banfield, at the King of Pruſſia, Marazion
Mr. Edmund Pearſe Banfill, Dartmouth
Mr. William Baſtard, Exeter, Coroner for the County of Devon. P. M.
Mr. S. Banton, Exeter
Mr. John Bate, Swan Inn and Tavern, at Poleſlor, near Exeter
James Barton, Eſq; St. James's Street, R. P.
Mr. Patrick Barry, Lymington
Mr. Henry Barrar, Little Park, Windſor
Mr. Bail, at the Flaſk, Chelſea
Mr. John Baker, of the Salutation Inn and Tavern, Topſham
Mr. Leopald Bachmire
Mr. Richard Barker, Surgeon, London, Royal Paper
Mr. John Barton, Architect, Wincheſter, R. P.
Mr. Richard Bethell, W. I. W. of the Paladian Lo. Hereford
Mr. Samuel Berry, Briſtol
Mr. Thomas Bennet, Glaſs-Maker, Briſtol
Mr. John Beard, Jun. Merchant, Penzance, P. M.
George Bell, Eſq; Falmouth, P. G. M.
Mr. Stephen Bell, ditto, R. W. M.
Mr. John Bearblock, Woollen Draper, Weſtminſter
Arthur Beardmore, Eſq; London
Mr. Birch, Wine Merchant, Bath
Mr. Biggs, Surveyor, at Windſor, R. P.
Mr. John Biggs, Butcher, at ditto
Mr. John Bidcock, Plymouth
Mr. Richard Martin Bird, Baker, Fenchurch Street
Mr. Thomas Blagden, Surgeon, Briſtol
Col. Blackwell, of the Glouceſterſhire Militia
Mr. William Blinch, Surgeon, Biddeford
Mr. Iſaac Blight, of the Salutation Lodge, Topſham
Mr. Blackamoor, Surveyor of Land, Devon
Mr. Pinkſtan Blackwood, Surgeon, W. J. W. of St. Alban's Lodge
Mr. James Blackwood, Old Jewry
Mr. Thomas Blachford, Lace Man, Lombard ſtreet
Mr. Daniel Blachford, ditto
John Blewett, Eſq; Marazian, Cornwall
Mr. Thomas Blewitt, Old King-Street, Briſtol
Mr. Edward Bowen, Linen Draper, Briſtol
Mr. Kichard Bowſher, White Hart ditto
Mr. Ephraim Booth, Plymouth

Mr. George Bowdige, of the Dragon Inn, Axminster
Theo. Bourke, Esq; Dartmouth Street, Westminster R. P.
James Boswell, Esq; Author of the History of Corsica
Mr. Francis Bowler, Master of an Academy, R. W. M.
Mr. John Bottomly, S. of St. Alban's Lodge
Mr. George Boulton, Charing Cross
Mr. J. Bowman, Gould Square, Crutched Fryars
Henry Toye Bridgeman, Esq; R. W. M. of the Corinthian Lodge, at Cardif, R. P.
Mr. George Bradford, W. S. W. of the Paladian Lodge, Hereford
Mr. John Brookes, P. M. Bath
Mr. William Browne, R. W. M. of the Lodge of Perfect Friendship, Bath
Mr. Elisha Bryne, Gun Maker, at Bristol
Mr. Edmond Bryan, W. S. W. of the Union Lodge ditto
Mr. Henry Brown, Tobacconist, Bristol
Mr. Andrew Brice, Printer, at Exeter, P. M.
Mr. Abraham Browne, Bookseller, at Bristol
Mr. John Brown, Mercer, at Evesham
Mr. John Bryan, Sculptor, at Painswick
Mr. Richard Bryce, of the Lodge at Topsham
Mr. Alexander Brice
Mr. Robert Bryant, Attorney at Law, Ilminster
Mr. John Braddon, Boot Tavern, Plymouth Dock
Lieut. P. Brustis, ditto
Mr. Michael Bradford, Surgeon, Launceston
Mr. James Bromley, Surgeon, at Poleslor, near Exon
Mr. John Brake, jun. Wine Merchant, at Crediton, P.M.
Mr. John Brutton, Haberdasher, Exon
Mr. Nicholas Brooke, Merchant, ditto
Mr. Samuel Bryant, Hosier, ditto
Mr. Thomas Bryer, King's-Arms Inn, Dorchester
Mr. Nathaniel Brookes, Merchant, Poole, Dorsetshire
Robert Brown, Esq; Manchester Buildings, Westminster, two Copies
George Brown, Esq; Bedford Street, R. Pa.
Thomas Browne, Esq; P. M. of St. George's Lodge, Taunton.
Mr. George Browne, Cavendish Street
Mr. Jos. Brown, of Long-Acre

Mr. Samuel Brawn, Castle Street
Matthew Brickdale, Esq; Member of Parliament, R. P.
Mr. William Brown, Watchmaker, Minories
Mr. Bradley, Carpenter, Long-Acre
Mr. Coun, Bush, P. M. of the Lodge of perfect Friendship, Bath
Mr. James Burr, Watchmaker, Bristol
Mr. W. Burton, R. W. M. Plymouth Dock
Mr. Charles Burdon, Attorney at Law, Black Torrington
Mr. John Burdon, at ditto
Mr. Thomas Burdon, Leather Dresser, Launceston
Mr. Richard Bungey, W. S. W. Salisbury
Mr. Robert Bussel, W. S. W. of St. George's Lodge, Exon
Mr. Thomas Bush, of Bradford, Wilts
John Buller, Esq; Member of Parliament, Roy. Pa.
Mr. John Bundy, Broad Street, P. M.
Mr. Atkinson Bush, Great Ormond Street
Mr. Ja. Burgess, Hosier, Coventry Street
Mr. Thomas Burrow, Fenchurch Street
Mr. Thomas Butler, Admiralty Office
Mr. Thomas Buckle, White Bear, Piccadilly

C

His Royal Highness the Duke of Cumberland, six Copies, Royal Paper
His Grace the Duke of Chandois 2 Cop. R. P.
The Right Hon. the Marquis of Carnarvan, four Copies, Royal Paper
The Right Hon. Lord Colville
Hon. Seymour Conway, R. P.
The Hon. William Craven, R. P.
Hon. General Colville, Bath
Mr. Carwardine, at Ledbury
Mr. Cambridge, at ditto
Mr. William Carey, Monmouth
Cor. Carpenter, Esq; Launceston
Captain Peter Carteret, of the Royal Navy, at Newton Abbot
Rev. Mr. Carne, at ditto
Mr. Samuel Cam, jun. Bradford, Wilts
Alexander Campbell, Esq; P. I. G. W. Royal Paper
Mr. Alexander Campbell, Sugeon, at Pool, R. W. M.
Mr. John Campbell, Cabinet-Maker, High Holbourn

Charles Carson, Esq; Lambeth, Royal Paper
Mr. Ison Cant, Glazier, Mary Le Bone
Mr. John Causeway, Brazier, Drury Lane
The Rev. Mr. Chalmers, P. M. of the Lo
Chelmsford
Mr. Jacob Chaille, merchant, Plymouth, P. M.
Mr. John Chease, P. M. Bristol
Mr. Richard Champion, Merchant at ditto
Mr. John Chandler, Coach-maker at ditto
Mr. Thomas Chaliner, Bridewell Precinct
Mr. Samuel Champion, Attorney at Law, Pl
R. W. M.
Henry Chittick, M. D. Marlborough Street
Rev. Mr. Cheer, Rector of White Booding, Ess
Mr. William Chapman, St. Martin's Lane
Mr. John Chapman, Spingfield, Essex
Mr. Childs, Silversmith, Winchester
Lieutenant Chaundy, in the Marines, Plymout
Lieutenant Christian of the Marines, ditto
Mr. Peter Clissold, Bristol
Mr. Rob. Clitsome, of Taunton, R. P.
Mr. Nicholas Clarke, at the Running Horse
Street, Westminster
Mr. James Clegg, Manchester, P. M.
J. Clarke, Esq; Saltash, Cornwall
Mr. Sam. Clarke, Mutton Cove, Plymouth Dock
Mr. David Cleak, Penzance, Surgeon
Mr. Noah Clift, New Inn, Dartmouth
Mr. John Clyde, Purser in the Navy
Mr. John Cleave, Exon, P. M.
John Stratford Collins, Esq; of the Vitruvian Lo
Mr. Thomas Collins, Hosier, Bath
Mr. Francis Collins, Union Lodge, Bristol.
Mr. Robert Collins, Brewer, at ditto
Mr. Robert Collins, Topsham, Devon, W. S.
Richard Cox, Esq; Bristol
Mr. David Cox, George Inn, Ilminster
R. H. Coxe, Esq; Member of Parliament, R.
Captain Cocks, of the Royal Navy, Plymouth
Mr. Peter Cocks, Gloucester
Mr. William Cock, at Plymouth
Mr. Thomas Court, Bristol
Mr. Philip Couch, jun. ditto
Mr. James Couch, of Newton Bushel, R. W. M.
Mr. Alexander Cowan, Plymouth Dock.
Lieutenant Robert Cowan, ditto

Mr. Robert Corker Penzance
Mr. John Cogdell, Great Gardens, St. Catharines
John Hart Cotton, Efq; two Copies, Royal Paper
Mr. William Cotton, Bedford Street, Covent-Garden
Rev. J. D. Cotton Vicar of Good Eafter, Effex
Mr. Abraham Cook, Silverfmith, Top of the Haymarket, P. M.
Mr. William Cook, Admiralty Office
Mr. WilliamCole, Engraver, Newgate-ftreet
Mr. Alexander Collmer, Peruke-Maker, Barnftaple
Captain George Collier, Oxford Road
Mr. Benjamin Collier, Ironmonger, ditto
Mr. Cofferet, Merchant, Exeter, R. W. M.
Mr. William Cooper, grocer, Caftle-ftreet, Oxford Road, W. S. W. of the Lodge of Regularity
Robert Cooper, jun. Efq; Salifbury
Mr. David Cooper, Pudding-Lane
Mr. John Colliholl, Brazier, Exeter
Mr. John Colborne, Notary Public at Poole, Dorfetfhire
Mr. Copleftone, Attorney at Law, Exeter, P. M.
Captain Carmouls, Warwick, Royal Paper
Mr. Charles Cowley, Golden Lion, Lynn Regis, Dorfet
Mr. Frederick Comyn, White Chapel
Colonel Craig, firft Groom of the Bed-Chamber to his Royal Highnefs the Duke of Cumberland, R. P.
Henry Crutchley, Efq; Royal Paper
William Cuthbertfon, Efq; Craven Buildings, R. P.

D

The Right Hon. Lord Vifcount Dudley, R. P.
George Durant, Efq; Member of Parliament, R. P.
Mr. James Davis, Landaff
Rev. Mr. John Davies, Rector of Grofmonant, Monmouthfhire
Mr. Markes Davies, Bath, P. M.
Mr. Charles Davies, Painter, Bath
Mr. William Danford, of the Union Lodge, Briftol
John Day, Efq; Cirencefter, Captain in the Gloucefterfhire Militia
Mr. Matthew Dawfon, Plymouth Dock
William Daw, Efq; Gatcombe, Devon
Mr. Charles Daire, Biddeford, ditto
Mr. William Daniel, Michael's Hill, Briftol

Mr.

Mr. ——— Davis, W. S. W. London
Mr. Charles Deering, of the Union Lodge, Bristol
Mr. William Derby, Plymouth
Mr. Abraham Freeman Dennis, Surgeon, at Crediton
The Lodge of Free-Masons at Deal, ten Copies
Mr. De Rippe, Baker, at Hammersmith
Mr. William Spicer Dix, Merchant, in Exeter
Mr. Dibsdale, at the Chequers Inn, Winchester
Mr. James Dixwell, Printer, St. Martin's Lane
Mr. George Downton, Mercer, Bath
Mr. William James Dodd, Bristol
Mr. Thomas Downie, at the Unicorn, Leominster
Mr. Michael Downes, Piccadilly
Mr. Alexander Dow, Great May's Buildings
Mr. John Drew, at Ledbury
Mr. Driver, Attorney, in Gloucester
Mr. Nathaniel Drake, Long-Acre
Mr. Dring, Feathers Tavern, Strand
Mr. John Dudley, Soapboiler, Gloucester
John Lenox Dutton, Esq; Captain in the Gloucestershire Militia
Mr. John Dunsford, Hot-press-man, St. George's Lodge, Exeter
Mr. John Durand, Shop-keeper, Hammersmith
Mr. William Dyer, Peruke-maker, Bath

E

The Right Hon. George Lord Edgcombe, Royal Paper
Mr. Jacob Easterbrooke, Bristol
Mr. John Eastcott, Surgeon, Launceston
W. B. Earle, Esq; Salisbury
William Earle, Esq; Chelsea, Royal Paper
Mr. Thomas Edwards, Holywell, P. M.
Mr. Richard Edwards, Watch-maker, Hereford
Mr. John Edwards, St. Ives, Cornwall
Peter Edwards, Esq; P. S. G. W.
Robert Eden, Esq; Piercy-street
Mr. John Edgar, Apothecary Salisbury
Mr. Elliot, at the Infirmary, Bath
John Errington, Esq; two Copies, Royal Paper
Mr. John Evans, Merchant at Carmarthen, South Wales, D. P. G. M. twelves Copies
Thomas Evans, Esq; of Penant, Brecknockshire.
Mr. Thomas Evans, Taylor, Holywell

Mr.

Mr. Thomas Evans, of Rumney, Glamorganshire
Mr. James Ewing, Brewer, Bath
Mr. Richard Evat, Upholsterer, Bath

F

Mr. J. J. Fabian, St. James's-street
Mr. James Faggotter, St. Ives, Cornwall
Mr. William Farley, Surgeon, Chudleigh, Devon
Mr. Farmer, Apothecary, Fleet-market
Mr. John Fear, Redcliff-street, Bristol
Mr. William Field, Attorney at Law, ditto
Mr. Pitman Scanderet Field, ditto
Mr. Fisher, Leicester-Fields
Mr. Thomas Flower, Bristol
Mr. William Fleming, Musician, Plymouth Dock
Mr. John Fleming, Exeter, W. I. W.
Mr. William Flamank, Newton Bushel, Devon]
William Fortune, Esq; Monmouth
Mr. Philip Foy, Bristol, W. J. W.
Mr. Robert Foot, Plymouth, R. W. M.
Mr. Josiah Foot, jun.
Mr. Austin Forest, Mercer, Plymouth
Mr. Joseph Ford, jun. Nursery-man, Exeter
Mr. William Fort, Sec. of the Amicable Lodge, ditto
Captain Fowkes, Equery to his Royal Highness the Duke of Cumberland, Royal Paper
Mr. John Forbes, Surgeon, Chelsea
Mr. Benjamin Foulston
Mr. Thomas Forsyth, Peruke-Maker, New Bond-street
Mr. Samuel Foyster, Tottenham-court-road
Napth. Franks, Esq, Great George-street, Westminster, Royal Paper
Mr. Edward Francis, Master of a Vessel
Mr. Thomas Frere, of the Thatched House Tavern, St. James's, Royal Paper
Mr. Joshua French, Horse-Fair, ditto
Mr. Fry, jun. Distiller, Bristol
Mr. Fricker, Pool, Dorsetshire
Mr. William Fryar, Exeter
Mr. John Fry, of the White-Hart Lodge, ditto

G

His Royal Highneſs the Duke of Glouceſter, ſix Copies, Royal Paper
The Right Hon. Lord Viſcount Gormanſton, R. P.
Sir Richard Glynn, Bart. Member of Parliament, R. P.
Mr. William Garnſey, Briſtol
Mr. Iſaac Garcia, Merchant, London
Mr. James Galloway, R. W. M. Pallmall
Mr. George Gally, Shug-Lane, P. M.
Mr. William Gardiner, R. W. M. of St. John's Lodge, Exeter
Mr. J. S. Gaudry, P. M. Bath, Royal Paper
Mr. Edward Gapp, Attorney at Law, Chelmsford
Mr. Samuel Geen, St. Ives, Cornwall
Mr. Daniel Gell, New-ſtreet, Devoſhire-ſquare
Mr. Joſeph Gerard, Plymouth
Mr. George Gilbert, of All Soul's Lodge, Tiverton
Captain Andrew Girardot, Royal Paper
Edward Gibbon, jun. Eſq; Royal Paper
Mr. S. Gillio, Surgeon
Mr. Robert Gill, jun. Attorney at Law, Doctor's Com.
Mr. William Gilborn, R. W. M. of the Lodge of Marines, Plymouth Dock
Mr. Goldney, Draper, at Bath
Mr. Edward Vernon Goodall, Attorney at Law, ditto
Mr. Alexander Gordon, Plymouth Tavern, Plymouth
Mr. Gough, Tallow-Chandler, Glanville-ſtreet
Mr. Goff, Surgeon, Pallmall
Mr. Lace Goodfellow, W. I. W. Saliſbury
Rev. Mr. Gower, Chelſea
Nathaniel Gould, Eſq; Colonel in the Guards, R. Pa.
Mr. John Griffiths, New-ſtreet, Covent-garden
Mr. Henry Gretton, Fenchurch-ſtreet
Mr. John Griffiths, Hoſier, Bond-ſtreet
Mr. Richard Gregory, Windſor
Rev. Mr. Gretton, Rector of Springfield, Eſſex
Lieutenant Andrew Grant, 22d Regiment of Foot
Mr. Henry Grinter, W. S. W. Amicable Lodge, Exeter
Mr. Philip Gregory, Mercer, Biddeford
Mr. Grundy, at the Green Dragon, Ledbury
Mr. Giles Greville, Surgeon, Briſtol
Mr. Patrick Graham, Union Punch-houſe, Briſtol
Mr. John Griffiths, on the Back, W. S. W. ditto

Mr. Edward Grumley, Mafh-ftreet, Briftol
Mr. James Grave, P. M. Purfer in the Royal Navy
Mr. John Griffiths, Plymouth-Dock
Mr. Jofeph Gregg, Plymouth
Mr. Thomas Green, Grocer, Launcefton
Mr. John Grenfell, Mercer, Penzance
Mr. James Gregory, Alresford
Mr. Charles Gullam, Houfe Painter, Briftol
Doct. Gufthart, Bath
M. Gunter, Green Dragon, Hereford
Captain John Gunning, Somerfet-houfe
Mr. William Gueft, Halfmoon-ftreet
Mr. John Gundry, Fountain-Court, Strand
Mr. Charles Gwavas, Merchant, Penzance
Rod. Gwynne, Efq; Deputy-Governor of Berwick Caftle
Marmaduke Gwynne, jun. Efq; Captain in the Radnorfhire Militia
John Gwatkin, Efq; Bullingham, near Hereford

H

Mr. Thomas Haviland, Apothecary, Bath
Mr. William Harford, Baker, ditto
Mr. James Hafkins, Briftol
Mr. Richard Hardwicke, Hereford
W. H. Hartley, Efq; Major in the Gloucefter Militia
Mr. John Hart, Merchant, London
Mr. Nathaniel Hart, Surgeon, Clerkenwell
Mr. George Harding, Apothecary, Strand
Mr. James Hardy, Clare-Market
Mr. Robert Harris, Druggift, St. Paul's Church-yard
Mr. Pymm Hammond, Carver, W. I. W of the Lodge of Regularity, London
Mr. Samuel Hayes, M. D. Lincoln's-inn-fields
Mr. William Hacket, Stafford
John Halliday, Efq; Banker, London, P. M.
Mr. Ifaac Hart, Great Pultney-ftreet, Golden-fquare
Mr. Zach. Hardman, Long-acre
Mr. Mofes Hart, ditto
Mr. John Hankins, ditto
Mr. John Harrifon, York
Mr. Edward Harvey, Plymouth-Dock
Mr. Robert Haydon, P. M. Plymouth

Mr. William Harrison, Gunner in the Royal Navy, Plymouth
Christopher Harris, Esq; Launceston, Cornwall
Mr. Edward Hambleton, of the Star Inn and Tavern, Marazion, Cornwall
Mr. John Hall, Limner, Marazion, ditto
Mr. Andrew Harward, Brazier, Totness, Devonshire
Mr. William Hatswell, St. John's Lodge, Exon
Mr. John Hawkins, W.J.W. of the White-Hart, Exeter
Mr. James Hart, Master of a Vessel
Charles Hanning, M. D. Crewkerne, Somersetshire
Mr. Isaac Harvey, Clothier, Axminster
Southcott Hallet, Esq; Dorsetshire
Mr. Samuel Alford Harbour, of the Bull-Inn, Bridport
Mr. John Haberdine, King's-Arms Lodge, Shad-Thames
Philip Hales, Esq; Lower Brook-street
Mr. Halford, Apothecary, Chelsea
Mr. Thomas Edward Harris, King-street
Mr. Henry Heath, P. M. Bristol
Mr. John Henderson, Tobacconist, Bristol
Mr. Thomas Hemburg, jun. ditto
Mr. S. Hewson, Apothecary, Mary-le-bone-street
Mr. James Heywood, Land-surveyor, St. Martin's-lane, R. W. M.
Mr. W. H. Heywood, Surgeon, Biddeford
Mr. Richard Hearne, Corner of Brooks-street, Holbourn
Mr. James Heseltine, Doctor's-Commons, R. P.
Isaac Head, Esq; Collector of the Customs at Scilly, R. P.
Mr. Alexander Hewet, at the Shoe-Warehouse, East-Smithfield
Mr. John Higgens, of the Lodge of Perfect Friendship, Bath
Mr. Roger Hicks, Seend, near Devizes, Wilts
Mr. James Hill, Bristol
Mr. John Hill, ditto
Mr. W. P. Hickling, Leadenhall Market
Mr. John Hinchcliffe, Stone-Mason, Long-acre
Mr. Nathaniel Hicks, W. J. W. St. Ives, Cornwall
Mr. Nathaniel Hicks, jun. St. Ives, ditto
Mr. William Hichens, Secretary, St. Ives Lodge, ditto
Mr. Robert Hibbs, Seven Stars, Totness
Mr. Aaron Hiscock, Exon
Mr. Josiah Hill, Plymouth-Inn, St. Thomas's, Exon
Mr. Philip Hill, Tawstock, Devonshire
Mr Samuel Hill, Anchor Smith, Topsham

Mr. Thomas Hill, Shipwright, ditto
Mr. John Hirst, Tower-hill
Rev. Mr. Hollings, Monmouth, Royal Paper
Mr. John Horton, Apothecary, Bath
Mr. John Hobbs, Bristol
Charles Holland, Esq; London
Mr. John Holdstock, Shirehampton
Mr. Thomas Hooper, Surgeon, P. M. Plymouth-Dock Lodge
Mr. Tyzack Hodges, Queen-Hythe
Mr. Richard Holloway, Crown and Anchor, Strand, Royal Paper
Mr. Henry Hoskyn, Launceston, Cornwall
John Hodges, Esq; Brook Street, Royal Paper
Rowland Holt, Esq; W. S. G. W. Royal Paper
Mr. Charles Hodder, King's-Arms Lodge, Shad-Thames
Mr. Robert Horn Homeward, W. S. W. Fair St. Horsleydown
John Hobson, Esq; Abington Buildings,
Mr. Joseph Holmden, Long-acre
Samuel Hughes, Esq; of the Monmouthshire Militia
Mr. Edward Hutchinson, Apothecary, Bath
Mr. James Hughes, Attorney at Law, Bristol
Mr. Robert Husband, Plymouth-Dock
Capt. Anthony Hunt, of the Royal Navy
Mr. William Hunt, Purser in the Royal Navy
Mr. William Hume, Plymouth
Rev. Mr. Thomas Hugo, Rector of Dunchidcock, Devonshire
Mr. John Hugo, Surgeon, Crediton
Mr. John Humphreys, Officer of the Excise, Salisbury
Mr. John Hughes, Hooper, Bristol
Mr. Mordecai, Hyams, ditto

J

Mr. Abraham James, Distiller, Bristol
Mr. Lazarus Jacobs, ditto
Mr. Richard James, Wine Merchant, Falmouth
Mr. George Jackson, of the Salutation Lodge, Topsham
Mr. William James, of the Royal Edwin Lodge, Lynn Regis
Mr. Jarrat, Pear-tree-street
Mr. Henry Jaffray, W. J. G. W. Royal Paper

George

George James, Esq; Soho
Mr. Samuel Jacemard, Oxford Road
Mr. Richard Jenn, Grocer, Plymouth Dock
Mr. Thomas Jefferson, St. John's Lodge, Exon
Captain Jennings, Gentleman of the Bed-chamber to the Duke of Cumberland
Mr. Henry Jefferies, P. M. Bristol
Mr. Thomas Jenner, Windsor
Mr. William Jelfe, New Palace Yard, Westminster
Mr. J. Jeffreys, Brewer, Hammersmith
Mr. Edward Iliffe, W. S. W. Union Lodge, Exon
Mr. Jones, Draper, Bath
Mr. Jolly, Perfumer, Bath
Mr. John Jones, Bristol
Mr. William Jones, Redcliffe-street, ditto
Mr. Gilbert Jones, Lower Bullingham, Herefordshire
Mr. James Johnson, Proctor of Hereford
Mr. John Jones, Chepstow, Monmouthshire
Mr. Robert Johnson, Plymouth-Dock
Mr. Thomas John, Merchant, Penzance
Richard Johns, Esq; Collector, Gweeke, Cornwall
Mr. Tremenheer Johns, Attorney at Law, Helstone, do.
Mr. Joseph Johnson, W. S. W. St. John's Lodge, Exeter
Robert Jones, Esq; Foumon Castle, Royal Paper
Mr. Francis Johnston, Brewer, New-street, near Broad-Street
Mr. George Jolliffe, Attorney at Law, Air-street, Piccadilly
William Johnston, Esq; Hammersmith
Mr. Robert Jones, Chelsea
Mr. John Johnston, May's Buildings
Mr. Thomas Jones, Long-acre
Mr. J. Judson, Great May's-Buildings
Henry Norton Ivers, Esq; Bath, two Copies

K

Mr. Frederick Kandler, of St. Alban's Lodge
Mr. Keene, Printer, Bath
Mr. William Kennelly, Plymouth Dock
Mr. John Keir, Surgeon, Marazion, Cornwall
Mr. Christopher Kempster, Chelsea
Mr. Daniel Keele, Watch-maker, Salisbury
John Keeling, Esq; Clerkenwell

Mr.

Mr. Robert Kellie, P. M. two Copies
Mr. Charles Keymys, Briſtol
Mr. Kitto, Bath
Mr. W. Kirkpatrick, of the Navy, Briſtol
Mr. George Kingdon, Hat-maker, Plymouth
Mr. William King, jun. Warebridge, Cornwall
Mr. James Kimpland, of the Fleece Inn and Tavern, Barnſtaple
Mr. William King, R. W. M. of the Cuſtom-houſe
John Knill, Eſq; P. M. of St. Ives
Lucy Knightly, Eſq; R. Pa.
Dr. Knox, Jermain-ſtreet, R. Pa.
Mr. Matthias Kulick, Surgeon, Lower Eaſt-Smithfield

L

The Right Hon. Earl of Leven, R. Pa.
Right Hon. Earl of Loudon, R. Pa.
The Hon. Robert Lee, Bath
Mr. William Lanſdown, Silverſmith, Bath
Mr. William Lane, of Launceſton
Rev. Mr. Thomas Lane, St. Ives Cornwall
Mr. Lane, Attorney at Law, King-ſtreet, Covent-Garden
Mr. Thomas Langdon, Long-acre
Mr. David Lambert, Malton, Yorkſhire
Mr. Joſeph Lawleſs, Exeter
Mr. Richard Langdon, Secretary of the Union Lodge, Exeter
Mr. William Langford, Hoppings, near Exeter
Mr. John Lander, Cuſtom-houſe, Pool, Dorſetſhire
Stephen Cæſar La Maiſtre, Eſq; Piercey-ſtreet
Mr. Thomas Lander, Eaton, Berks, P. M.
Mr. J. Laverick, Piccadilly
Mr. David Lambert
Mr. Lewis, Proctor, Landaff
Mr. Thomas Leach, Surgeon, at Chepſtow
Mr. Thomas Lewis, Secretary of the Vitruvian Lodge at Roſs, Herefordſhire
Mr. Thomas Llewellin, Fiſhmonger, Briſtol
Mr. Step. Lewis, Gay-ſtreet, ditto
Mr. John Lean, ditto
Mr. J. Lewis, Attorney at Law, Plymouth, P. M.
Mr. George, Taylor, Plymouth, P. M.
Mr. Charles Leadbetter, Jeweller, Carey-Lane, London
Mr. John Leer, Attorney at Law, W. S. W. Pool, Dorſet

Samuel Lewin, Esq; Chelmsford
Mr. James Leishman, W. S. W. Minories, R. P.
Mr. Thomas Lewling, Rupert-street
George Leg, Esq;
Mr. John Lilly, Falmouth
Mr. Thomas Linfoot, Cross-lane, Long-acre
John Lloyd, Esq. Cwmbrane, Carmarthenshire
Mr. Lowdon, Apothecary, Bristol
Mr. S. Lorrimore, ditto
Mr. Henry Loveday, sen. Painswick
Mr. Thomas Lloyd, Plymouth
Captain Logan, of the Marines, ditto
Edward Lovel, Esq; Windsor-Castle, R. Pa.
Captain Jacob Lobb, Penzance
Mr. Loveday, Apothecary, Hammersmith
Mr. William Lodder, the Lion and Lamb Inn, Pool, Dorsetshire
Rev. Mr. Lock, W. J. W. Union Lodge, Exeter
Mr. Samuel Luscombe, Surgeon, Exeter, 2 Copies
Mr. John Luckcombe, Tr. of St. George's Lo. Exon
Mr. Steph. Luke, Merchant, W. J. W. Penzance
Mr. George Lyne, Mercer, Launceston
Mr. Christopher Lymebear, Fountain Inn, Oakhampton, Devon
Captain Lynch, of the 22d Regiment Treasurer of the Union Lodge, Exeter
Mr. Alex. Lyall, Kings Arm's Lodge, Shad Thames
Capt. Thomas Lynn, of the Royal Navy, 2 Copies
Mr. John Joseph Lyon, Hope Tavern, Horsley-down

M

Right Hon. Lord Vis. Molyneux, 2 Copies, Ro. Pa.
Sir. Alex. Mc'Donald, Bart.
Mr. Daniel Mansfield, W. J. W. of the Vitruvian Lodge at Ross
Mr. Humphrey Matthews, of the Vitruvian Lodge at Ross
Mr. Maagee, Statuary, Bath
Mr. James Richard Maud, Bristol
Mr. John Merchant, Redcliffe-street, Bristol
Mr. Richard Broad, Manning, Three Crowns, Plymouth
Mr. Richard Mac'Gannon, of the Plymouth Division of Marines

Mr.

Mr. Richard Maltby, Wine Merchant, James-ſtreet, Long-Acre
Rev. Mr. H. C. Manley, Bradninch, Devon
Thomas Maſters, Eſq; Royal Paper
Mr. Geo. Woodward Mallet, Attorney at Law, Plymouth
Lieut. Mc'Kenzie, 43d Regiment of Foot, Plymouth
Lieut. Mc'Neil, of the Marines, Plymouth
Mr. John Manning, Brazier, Launceſton
Mr. Thomas Mc'Lellan, Falmouth
Mr. Robert Martin, Launceſton, 2 Copies
Lieut. Charles Mac Lean, of the 43d Regiment
Mr. Mac Auſland, Merchant, Plymouth Dock
Mr. John Marnell, Plymouth Dock-yard
Mr. Nicholas May, Surgeon, Plymouth-Dock
Mr. Phillip Matthew, Attorney at Law, Chudleigh, Devonſhire
Lieutenant William Marler, Exon
Mr. Samuel Mayne, Hot-preſſer, St. John's Lodge, Exeter
Mr. Benjamin Mace, Surgeon, 22d Regiment, 2 Copies
Mr. Richard Mallock, Writing-Maſter, Axminſter
Mr. Robert Mapſon, King's-Arms Lo. Shad Thames
Joſ. Mauger, Eſq; Member of Parliament, R. Pa.
L. M' Leane, Eſq; two Copies, R. Pa.
Mr. Henry John Maſkall, Apothecary, Oxford Road, R. W. M.
Mr. James M' Clary, Windſor, P. M.
Mr. Robert Maſon, Change-Alley
Mr. John Maſon, Woollen-draper, Briſtol
Mr. Thomas Maxfield, Toy-maker, ditto
Mr. Matthew Meaſe, jun. ditto
Mr. John Meaiſey, Wincheſter
Mr. Thomas Mercer, S. Poole
Mr. Thomas Martin, of the King's-Arms Lodge, Shad-Thames
Mr. John Mills, Briſtol
Mr. Stephen Millet, St. James's Back
Mr. J. Milton, jun. Cuſtom-houſe, Briſtol
Richard Michens, Eſq; Penzance
John Michie, Eſq; Spring-gardens, R. Pa.
Mr. Iſaac Miſaubin, St. Martin's-Court
Rev. Mr. Ja. Minifie, of Fairwater, Sommerſetſhire
Mr. Edward Minifie, London
Mr. James Miſt, Ironmonger, Long-acre
Mr. Henry Morgan, Rumney, near Cardiffe

Mr. Lewis Morgan, Rumney, near Cardiffe
Mr. Edmond Morton, Coach-maker, Bath
Mr. Edward Morgan, P. M. of the Pythagoric Lodge, Briſtol
Mr. William Morgan, Leather-dreſſer
Mr. Samuel Moore, St. Peter's Hoſpital, Briſtol
Mr. Thomas Moore, Guinea-ſtreet, ditto
Mr. Thomas Mountjoy, Wine-hooper, ditto
Mr. John Morſe, Accomptant, ditto
Mr. Edward Moffett, Painter, Temple-Lane
Mr. William Moore, Hereford
Mr. Paul Mounier, Attorney at Law, Plymouth Dock Lodge, P. M.
Mr. D. Morris, Queen of Bohemia's Head, Wych-ſtreet
Mr. R. Moody, Fiſhmonger, Leadenhall-Market
Mr. F. Morgan, Optician, Ludgate-ſtreet
Mr. J. Mounier, Surgeon, Plymouth
Mr. Job. Brookes Moone, Plymouth-Dock
Captain Moleſworth, of the 43d Regiment, Plymouth
Mr. Alexander Moſes, Falmouth
Mr. James Morton, of the King's-Arms Lodge, Shad-Thames, R. W. M.
Mr. George Moore, Windſor
Mr. Nathaniel Mullens, Goldſmith, Briſtol
Mr. John Mullens, the George, David-ſtreet
Mr. Stephen Munden, Fleet-ſtreet
Mr. Charles Munden, Windſor
Mr. James Muſſard, Coal-Merchant
Mr. William Munden, Chelſea
Mr. H. Munro, Conduit-ſtreet

N

Mr. James Nayler, Croſs-Keys, Mary le Bone Lane
Mr. Robert Newman, Surgeon, R. W. M. of the Vitruvian Lo. at Roſs, Herefordſhire
Mr. Adam Newman, Innholder, Bath
Mr. John Netterville, Temple-Croſs, Briſtol
Mr. Felix Neale, Briſtol
Mr. Richard Nelſon, Mercer, Plymouth Dock, P. M.
Lieut. Joſ. Neville, of the Royal Navy, Plymouth
Mr. George Nelſon, Gatcombe, Devonſhire
Mr. Holdſworth Newman, W. S. W. of the Lodge, Dartmouth
Mr. Gilbert Neyle, Exon,

Mr. Obadiah Newell, Master of a Vessel
Mr. James Newey, Custom-house, London
Mr. Thomas Nevell, Sweedland-court
Mr. Thomas Neale, Mary-le-bone
Tho. Nichols, Esq; S. W. of the Vitruvian Lodge, Ross
Mr. Jonathan Noad, Bristol
Mr. Tho. North, R. W. M. of the Jerusalem Lodge, do.
Mr. P. Norton, Wine-street, ditto
Mr. William Northcote, Surgeon, Cornwall
Mr. Nowell, of the Fountain Inn and Tavern, Taunton

O

C. Ogilvy, Esq; two Copies, R. Pa.
Mr. D. Ogilvy, Surgeon, Cursitor-street, Chancery-lane
Mr. John Ogilvie, Conduit-street, W. J. W.
John Ommanney, Esq; Plymouth
Mr. Jos. Oldfield, York
Mr. Edward Onion, at the Bull, High-street, Bristol
Mr. Peter Ougier, Dartmouth
Hugh Owen, Esq; Lower Grosvenor-street
Mr. Thomas Owen, Hatter, Bristol
Mr. Francis Owen, Cabinet-maker, Bristol
Captain A. Owen, of the Foot Guards
Mr. John Owen, Officer of Excise, Monmouth, P. M.
Mr. John, Oxley, Gardener, Bristol

P

Sir Richard Phillipps, Bart. Member of Parliament, R. P.
The Paladian Lodge, Hereford, ten Copies
Francis Paget, Esq; at the Cocoa-tree Coffee-house
Mr. John Palmer, P. M. of the Lodge of Perfect Friendship, Bath
Mr. Palmer of the Pelican, Bristol
Mr. Peter Pardoe, ditto
Mr. Robert Paul, Surgeon, Ilminster
Mr. Jos. Parfett, Baker, Carnaby-market
Mr. Thomas Parkinson, King's-Head Tavern
Mr. Jos. Parsloe, of the New Marlbro' Coffee-house, Great Marlbrough-street
George Palmer, Esq; R. W. M. York, Royal Paper
Michael Henry Pascall, Captain in the Royal Navy
Mr. James Parsons, Merchant, Plymouth
Mr. William Parry, Taylor, ditto

Mr. John Parker, Leather-dresser, Launceston
Mr. David Palmer, of Do.
Mr. Anthony Page, jun. Barnstaple
Mr. John Place, of Pilton
Mr. James Partridge, Exon
Mr. John Paulyn, Exon
George Patterson, Esq; Great Marlbrough-street, R. P.
John Parker, Esq; Member of Parliament, R. P.
John Patterson, Esq; Burlington-street, two Copies, Royal Paper
Mr. J. D. Parker, Chelmsford
John Pattinson, Esq; London
Peter Paumier, Esq; Do. R. Pa.
Capt. Pascall, of the Royal Navy
Mr. Anthony Parquot, Wardour-street
Mr. John Pattinson, Great Rider-street, St. James's
Mr. William Perry, Boston, New-England
Mr. Charles Peer, Quarter-master Serjeant of Marines, W. S. W. Plymouth Dock
Mr. Perkin's, Brawn's-Head, Bond-street
Mr. Peters, Portrait Painter, Wellbeck-street, 6 Copies
Mr. William Pearse, W. S. W. Bath
Mr. John Redley, Dean's-court, Doctor's Commons
Mr. John Pearce, Surgeon, Penzance
Mr. Thomas Penrose, P. M. Attorney at Law, ditto
Mr. William Pendar, Surgeon, Falmouth
Mr. Thomas Pering, W. J. W. Dartmouth
Mr. William Penny, Surgeon, P. M. Newton-Abbot
Mr. Richard Pearce, Biddeford
Mr. Edward Perry, Free-Mason's Arms, Poleslar, near Exon
Mr. John Perkins, Serge-maker, Amicable Lodge, Exeter, P. M.
Mr. James Peacock, King's-Arms, Shad Thames
Mr. Samuel Penistone, Bird-street
Mr. Ansley Pellatt, W. J. W. St. John-street, R. P.
Mr. Edward Phillips, Attorney at Law, Gloucester
Mr. James Phillips, Secretary at the Rose and Crown, Custom-house
James Phipps, Esq; R. P.
Rev. Mr. Pitman, Hereford, R. P.
Mr. William Pichard, Water-gilder, Little Old Bailey
Mr. William Pinckney, St. Paul's-church-yard
Mr. Fleming Pinkstan, Surgeon, P. M.
Mr. John Pinkey, Surgeon, Dartmouth

Mr.

Mr. John Place, Pilton
Mr. James Poole, Esq; Taunton
William Richards, Powell, Esq; of Cardiffe Lodge
Mr. William Powell, of the Paladian Lodge, Hereford.
Mr. William Powell, Bristol
Mr. William Powell, of the Union Lodge, ditto
Mr. Robert Poole, Watch-maker, Aldersgate-street
Mr. Pohl, Great Maddox-street
Mr. Henry Pollexfen, Ship-Inn, Newton Bushel, Devonshire
Mr. Hugh Powell, Barnstaple
Mr. Amb. Pinney, of the Amicable Lodge, Exon
John Carter Pollard, Esq; R. P.
Mr. John Pott, St. James's
Capt. Price, Watford, Glamorganshire
Mr. Richard Priest, Cardiffe
Rev. Mr. John Price, Bristol
Mr. William Price, Linen-draper, Norwich
Mr. William Priest, Watch-maker, Bristol
Mr. Peter Prigg, Carpenter, ditto
Mr. James William Preston, Botolph-lane
J. P. Pryse, Esq; Member of Parliament, R. P.
Mr. Richard Prior, jun. Butcher-row, London
Mr. E. Price, Silversmith, R. W. M. Ludgate-street
Mr. Francis Prior, P. M. Plymouth
J. Price, Esq; Penzance, two copies
Mr. John Price, Accomptant, Bristol
Mr. William Pride, Goldsmith, Salisbury
Mr. Charles Prater, Baker
Mr. Thomas Preston, Dufours-court, Broad-street, Golden-square
Mr. Purdie, Spring-gardens, Bath
Mr. Charles Pugh, Bookseller, Hereford
Mr. H. Pulsford, St. Martin's-lane
Mr. James Puddicombe, Newton Bushell
Mr. William Purchase, Crediton
Benjamin Pugh, M. D. Chelmsford, P. M.
Mr. Pyne, Post-master, of Bristol
Mr. Samuel Pye, Surgeon, ditto
Mr. Benjamin Pyke, of the Golden Lion Inn and Tavern, Barnstaple
Robert Hampden Pye, Esq; Audley-street, R. P.
Mr. Maurice Pugh, Chelmsford, Surgeon

R

Colonel Rainsford, Equery to his Royal Highness the Duke of Gloucester
Mr. John Rawlings, Plymouth Dock, P. M.
Mr. William Rae, Woollen-draper, Cranbourne-alley
Mr. Jos. Randill, Surgeon, Brownlow-street
Mr. John Ratcliffe, Glass-worker, Bristol
Mr. Randal, Butcher, Hammersmith
Mr. John Vining, Reade, Portsmouth, P. M.
Mr. Thomas Reynolds, one of the Coroners for the County of Devon, at Plymouth
Mr. Luke Reilley, Lincoln's-Inn
Mr. George Redaway, Crediton, Devon
William Reynolds, Esq; Coroner for the County of Essex, P. M.
Mr. George Reynolds, Rose and Crown, opposite the Custom-house
Mr. John Reynolds, at ditto
Mr. Thomas Read, jun. Bristol
Mr. John Ric, Sugar Baker, ditto
Richard Ripley, Esq; P. S. G. W. Royal Paper
Horatio Ripley, Esq; P. S. G. W.
Mr. John Ridge, Taylor, Plymouth
J. B. Rich, Esq; Cecil-street, London, R. P.
John Richardson, jun. Esq; Piercy-street, R. P.
Mr. Benjamin Rinch, Painter, Plymouth
Mr. Samuel Rickards, Miniature Painter, Poland-street
Mr. Ja. Richards, Maiden Down, Devonshire
Mr. Richard Richardson, Stock-broker, in the Strand
Mr. John Rigge, Attorney at Law, Inner-Temple, R. W. M.
Mr. John Roberts, of the Union Lodge, Bristol
Mr. Marmaduke Roberts of ditto
Mr. John Rogers of ditto
Mr. Edward Rooke, Organist of All-Saints, Bristol
Mr. John Rowand, Linen-draper, ditto
Mr. Richard Rowdon, Attorney at Law, Plymouth-Dock
Mr. William Rowe, Surgeon, Launceston
Francis Rod, Esq; of Trebartha-hall, Cornwall
Mr. Peter Rogers, School-master, Launceston
Mr. Thomas Robyns, Attorney at Law, Marazian, Cornwall
Mr. Roger Rose, of the Lodge of Perfect Friendship, Bath

Lieut.

Lieut. Col. John Roberts, Taunton, R. P.
Rev. Mr. James Roberts, of Linton, Herefordſhire
Mr. William Rogers, Brandy Merchant, Monmouth
Mr. Thomas Rogers, Watchmaker, Bath
Mr. James Roe, James-ſtreet, Covent-garden
Mr. William Roſs, P. M. of the Lodge at the Feather's Tavern, Strand
Mr. Geo. Rous, Goldſmith, Noble-ſtreet, Foſter-lane
Mr. William Roberts, Hoſier, Jermyn-ſtreet
Mr. John Roberts, Hoſier, Newgate-ſtreet
Mr William Roſe, Buffalo Tavern, Bloomſbury
Mr. James Rowe, Baker, Lower Thames Street
Mr. Thomas Rodda, Cabinet-maker, Marazian
Mr. Samuel Rodda, Merchant, at ditto
Mr. George Rooke, Barnſtaple
Mr. Edward Roebuck, Swallow Street
Mr. Paul Roubel, W. J. W. of the Lodge of Perfect Friendſhip, Bath
Mr. William Roberts, Iſleworth
Mr. John Rogers, Craig's-court, Charing-croſs
Mr. Henry Rowe, Falmouth
Mr. Ruſpini, Pallmall
Mr. James Ruſhen, R. W. M. 22d Regiment of Foot
Mr. George Ruſſel, Chelſea
Mr. James Ryan, Surgeon, at Briſtol

S

Colonel St. Leger, Roy. Pa.
Mr. Robert Savours, Mercer, Cardiffe
Mr. Peter Salmon, Taylor, Bath
Mr. Charles Sawyer, Union Lodge, Briſtol P. M.
Mr. William Sayer, Treaſurer, Little Tower-hill
Mr. Thomas Sanſon, P. M. Eaſt-Smithfield
Mr. Humphrey Sawden, Chelſea
Mr. Chriſtopher Saltren, R. W. M. Launceſton
Mr. John Saltren, Biddeford
Mr. Samuel Sanders, Poleſlar, Exon
Mr. John Saliſbury, Joiner and Cabinet-Maker, do.
Francis Salvador, Eſq; Dover-ſtreet, R. P.
Mr. James Scholefield, London, R. P.
Mr. James Science, Barnſtaple
Mr. William Scott, St. John's Lodge, Exon
James Scawen, Eſq; Member of Parliament, R. P.
Dr. Schomberg, Bath

D. Scrafton, Esq; Chelmsford
John Scawen, Esq; Rider-street
Mr. Pieter, Scheidechyer, South-audley-street
Mr. John Searle, jun. Chudleigh
Mr. Walter Prynne Seth, W. S. W. Exeter
Mr. Shrowsbridge, Watch-maker, Albion's-buildings, Bartholomew-close
Mr. James Sheridine, R. W. M. Mary-le-bone
Mr. Shiercliffe, Bristol
Molineux Shuldham, Esq; Plymouth
Lieutenant Richard Shea, Plymouth
Mr. Thomas Sheppard, Newton Bushell
Robert Shastoe, Esq; R. P.
Mr. Samuel Sheers, Surgeon, Bristol
Mr. Joseph Shapland, Apothecary, ditto
Mr. Thomas Shapland, Tobacconist, ditto
Mr. Alex. Shedden, Secretary of the Union Lodge, do.
Mr. John Shute, W. S. W. of St. George's Lodge, Taunton
Mr. Thomas Sweeting, Attorney at Law, Sec. of St. George's Lo. Taunton
Mr. William Sheppard, Secretary, Lymington
Mr. Thomas Shaw, Surgeon, Windsor
Mr. John Shield, Gloucester-house
Mr. J. Sheppard, Charing-cross
Mr. William Sheppard, Oxford-street
Mr. John Sieban, Ironmonger, Bristol
Mr. Richard Simpson, Apothecary, ditto
Mr. Hump. Simmons, Stationer, Chancery-lane
Thomas Singleton, Esq, P. S. G. W.
Mr. D. Sill, Austin-Fryars
Mr. Simpson, Taylor, Rolle's Buildings
Major Skey, of the 43d Regiment of Foot, Plymouth
Mr. Thomas Skinner, Secretary, Dartmouth
Mr. Highmore Skeats, R. W. M. Salisbury
Mr. William Slocombe, Bristol
Mr. John Sloman, Malster, Newton Bushell
Mr. Smith Tobacconist, Red Lion Street
Mr. Samuel Smith, Agent, Tower Street
Mr. John Smith, Mark-lane
John Smith, Esq; Hammersmith, R. W. P. G. M. Royal Paper
Mr. John Smith, Fishmonger, St. Paul's Church-yard
Mr. William Smith, St. Martin's-lane, P. M.
Mr. Martin Smith, of the College, Gloucester

Mr.

Mr. William Smith, Attorney, in Ilminster
Mr. Thomas Smith, Ilforde Combe
Mr. William Smale, jun. W. S. W. of All Soul's Lodge, Tiverton
Mr. George Smith, Attorney at Law, Axminster
Mr. Joshua Smith, W. S. W. Lynn Regis
Mr. Smith, Confectioner, Bath
John Smith, Esq; Hammersmith, P. G. M.
Mr. Smith, Attorney at Law, Bath
Mr. Richard Smith, Bristol
Mr. John Smith, ditto
Mr. John Smily, Castle-street, ditto
John Smith, Esq; Member of Parliament, R. P.
Mr. Thomas Smith, Carpet Warehouse, Temple-bar
Mr. Robert Smith, St. Paul's Church-yard
Mr. Snailon, Bath
Mr. Robert Snooke, Upholder, of Dorchester
Mr. Edward Snoxell, Falmouth
Richard Spicer, Esq; London
Mr. William Spencer, York
Mr. William Spowers, St. Stephen's, near Launceston, Cornwall
Mr. Robert Sparke, Merchant, Dartmouth
Mr. Thomas Spyring, Exeter
Mr. Joshua Springer, P. M. Bristol
Mr. Samuel Spencer, Sadler, Fenchurch-street
Mr. Joseph Squire, Merchant, Plymouth
Mr. R. Stevenson, Tobacconist, Strand
Mr. J. Stephens, Stone-mason, Long-acre
Mr. William Strong, Queen's-Head, Mary-le-bone
Mr. Steel, Baker, Fleet-street
John Stephens, Esq;
Mr. George Strong, Apothecary, St. Thomas's, Exon
Mr. John Sturtridge, of the White-hart Lodge, ditto
Mr. William Stephens, Sadler, ditto
Mr. Thomas Stickland, Attorney, Dorchester
Mr. Thomas Stephens, Wine-merchant, Poole
Sir Frank Standish, Bart. Member of Parliament, R. P.
Thomas Stapleton, Esq; two Copies, R. P.
Mr. John Stephens, of Plymouth-Dock Lodge
Mr. William Strange, Plymouth
Mr. William Stephens, P. M. St. Ives, Cornwall
Mr. John Stone, Penzance, ditto
Mr. Nath. Steele, Ironmonger, Falmouth
Mr. Jos. Stapleton, Dartmouth

Rev. James Stonhouse, M. D. Bristol
Rev. James Stonehouse, L. L. D. two Copies
Capt. Thomas Stonhouse, Madrass, East-Indies
Mr. John Stone, Cardiffe
Rev. Dr. Stone, Hereford
Mr. William Street, Apothecary, Bath
Mr. Benj. Stevenson, Bristol
Mr. Thomas Stokes, Attorney at Law, Plymouth
Mr. William Stacey, Braintree
Phil. Sturgeon, Esq; Captain in the Essex Militia
Mr. George Stubbs, Warwick-street, Charing-cross
Mr. Abraham Stiles, Secretary
Mr. John Starkey, Broad-street, Carnaby-market
——— Stark, M. D. Princes-street
Mr. John Strahan, Doctor's Commons
Mr. Thomas Sweeting, Attorney at Law, Taunton
Mr. Ja. Sweetnam, Small-street
Mr. Charles Sweetland, St. George's-Lodge, Exon
Mr. Hugh Sweetland, of all Soul's Lodge, Tiverton
Mr. Abraham Symonds, Plymouth-dock
Mr. William Symonds, jun. Hereford
Mr. Thomas Symonds Sculptor, Hereford
Mr. Francis Symonds, Penzance

T

Sir Charles Kemys Tynte, Bart. Member of Parliament, R. P.
John Tempest, Esq; Member of Parliament, R. P.
David Tanner, Esq; Monmouth
The Rev. Mr. Taswell, Hereford
Mr. Taylor, Bookseller, Bath, W. J. W.
Mr. Roger Tatam, Bristol
Mr. Richard Taylor, Tobacconist, Gloucester
Mr. John Tasker, Mercer, York
Mr. John Taylor, P. M. Pool, Dorsetshire
Mr. Charles Taylor, New-Exchange, Strand, P. M.
Mr. Thomas Taylor, Brewer, King-street, Golden-square
Mr. Tho. Mem. Thorn, Silversmith, Plymouth-dock, P.M.
Mr. Henry Thomas, Brewer, Plymouth
Lieut. William Thorne, of the 43d Regiment
Mr. Samuel Thorpe, Distiller, Wardour-street, Soho, R.P.
Mr. William Thompson, Butcher, Clare-market
Mr. Benj. Thornton, Haddock's Bagnio, Royal Paper
Mr. Thredder, Coach-maker, Wells-street, Oxford-road
Mr. Alex. Third, Hatter, Strand

Mr.

Mr. Thompſon, Upholder, Fenchurch-ſtreet
Mr. Matthew Thomas, of the Paladian Lodge, Hereford
Mr. John Thomas, of Coedy-goraſs, Glamorganſhire
Mr. Tilſed, Sail-maker, Poole, Dorſet
Mr. Charles Tindal, Briſtol
Mr. James Tovey, Surgeon, Penzance
John Townſon, Eſq; Southampton-Buildings, R. P.
Mr. Mark Tool, Chelſea
Rev. Jacques Touzeau, Plymouth
Mr. Joſeph Troughton, Silkman, Briſtol
Mr. Rob. Trent, Surgeon, Ilminſter
Mr. John Trengrouſe, of St. Ives, Cornwall, W.S.W.
Mr. Tregurtha, Merchant, Penzance, R.W. M.
Mr. Wm. Tremenheer, Attorney at Law, ditto, W.S.W.
Mr. Nicholas Triſt, Grocer, Totneſs
Mr. William Tringham, Engraver, Fleet-ſtreet
Mr. Thomas Tremlett, jun. Dartmouth
Mr. Andrew Tracey, Mariner, ditto
Capt. J. Treby, of his Majeſty's Army, Chudley, Devon
Mr. Thomas Treſlove, jun. St. Martin's-lane
John Trent, Eſq; two Copies, R. Pa.
Pregrine Treves, Eſq; Merchant, London, R. P.
Mr. Nicholas Tucker, Painter, Bath
Mr. William Tucker, at the Greyhound and Shakeſpear Inn and Tavern, Bath
Mr. Richard Tucker, of Tiverton, Devon
Mr. George Tucker, Ironmonger, Axminſter
Mr. John Tucker, Linen-draper, ditto
Mr. Fryer Tucker, Exeter
Rev. Mr. Tucker, Lyme-Regis, Dorſetſhire, 2 Copies, R. W. M.
Mr. John Tuff, of ditto, W. S.W.
Mr. Edward Turner, Chelſea
Mr. Thomas Turner, Dyer, St. George's Lodge, Exeter
Lieut. Col. Twiſtleton, R. P.

U

Mr. Underwood, of Hereford, P. M.
Rev. Mr. Underwood, of ditto
Mr. James Upham, Topſham, Devon
Mr. William Uſtick, Mercer, Marazian

V

William Vaughan, Eſq; P. G. M. for North-Wales
Col. Van Teylingen, four Copies, R. P.

Mr. Thomas Lewelling Vining, Bristol
Mr. James Vivian, Assistant at Mr. Downes's Academy Bristol
Mr. Rumbelow Vivian, Surgeon Falmouth
Mr. William Vincent, Dorchester

W

The Right Hon. Lord Viscount Wenman, R. P.
The Right Hon. Lord Waltham, R. P.
Sir Watkin Williams Wynn, Bart. four Copies, R. P.
Sir Thomas Worsley, Bart. two Copies, R. P.
Robert Boyle Walsingham, Esq; Member of Parliament, P. G. M. Royal Paper
Major Edward Walpole, R. P.
Mr. Thomas Walner, Bristol
Francis Swaine Ward, Esq; Broad-street
Mr. Wm. Wallace, White-Hart, Five Fields, Chelsea
Mr. Wade, Watch-maker, Great Brook-street
Mr. John Way, Bath
Mr. Richard Walker, Windmill-street
Mr. Waters, Carpenter, in the Strand
Mr. Thomas Watkinson, Tower
Mr. Peter Warren, Exchange-alley
Mr. James Wallis, Bookseller, Plymouth
Mr. Jacob Watson, Church-Tavern, Plymouth-Dock
Mr. Wallis, St. Ives Lodge, Cornwall
Mr. Christopher Wallis, Penzance
Mr. Francis Walker, Woollen-draper, Great Torrington
Mr. William Walker, Exeter
Mr. James Warsham, Peruke-maker, Bristol
Mr. Thomas Warren, Tiverton
Mr. John Walker, Surgeon, in the 22d Regiment
Mr. John Wady, Jeweller, Bristol
John Wallis, Esq; Clerk of the Peace of Dorsetshire
Mr. Samuel Watkinson, Butcher, St. Mary-le-bone
Mr. William Watts, Hooper, Bristol
John Webb, Esq; P. M. Cavendish-square
Mr. Samuel Webber, at Topsham
Mr. Richard Welland, Master of a Vessel
Mr. John Weech, Treasurer, All Souls Lodge, Tiverton
Mr. Richard Webb, of the Soap-house, Bristol
Mr. Weaver, Barton-street, Bristol
Mr. James Welsh, City Marshal, Bristol
Mr. William Wellick, Coach-maker, Bristol

Mr.

Mr. Robert Weatherley, Printer, Plymouth
Mr. Phillip Weſtcott, W. S. W. Falmouth
Mr. Henry Weir, Deputy Pay-Maſter of the Marines.
Mr. John Weſtlake, Serge-maker, Leſt Withiel
Mr. Weſt, Apothecary, Bath
Mr. John Webb, W. S. W. Briſtol
Mr. Welch, Cheſterfield-houſe
Mr. Peter Wells, Surgeon, Briſtol
Mr. John Whitmaſh, R. W. M. of St. George's Lodge, Taunton
Mr. Henry Whitmaſh, of ditto
Mr. Joſ. White, at the Talbot, Bath
Mr. Zacheriah Whiting, W. S. W. Briſtol
Mr. Hugh Whitaker, R. W. M. Ruſſel-court
Mr. Timothy Wheelwright, W. J. W. Falmouth
Mr. Nathaniel Wiſe, Union Lodge, Briſtol
Mr. John Williams, Book-keeper, ditto
Mr. William Wigginton, Toyman, ditto
Mr. James Williams, Cornfactor, ditto
Mr. Michael Wills, Change-broker, ditto
Mr. Gilbert Williamſon, Sec. of the Lo. at the Duke of Beaufort's Head, ditto
Mr. George Winter, Linen-draper, ditto
Thomas Willoughby, Eſq; Dublin
Mr. Henry Willoughby, of Northweek, in Somerſetſhire
Henry Williams, Eſq; Crickhowell, Brecknockſhire
Mr. Henry Wintle, Glouceſter
Mr. John Winter, Plymouth-dock
Joſ. Willis Eſq; Mayor of Saliſbury, P. M.
Capt. George Wiſe of Poole, Dorſet
Mr. Wiſe, of Lymington
Robert Wilſon, Eſq; Weſtminſter
Mr. Charles Wigan, Diſtiller, Charing-croſs
Mr. Richard Willbor, York
Mr. John Williams, Stationer, Fleet-ſtreet
Mr. Wilburn, Grocer, Hammerſmith
Mr. John Williams, Pembroke
Mr. Henry Williams, Mercer of Cardiffe
Mr. William Williams, Stationer, Monmouth
Mr. Thomas Wilkins, of the Fryars, near Newport, Monmouthſhire.

Mr. William Winston, Watch-maker, R. W. M. of the Paladian Lodge, Hereford
John Williams, Esq; Wimpole-street
Mr. William Williams, Carver and Gilder, Bristol
Mr. Charles Williams, Taylor, ditto
Mr. John Wise, at ditto
Mr. Nathaniel Windey, Attorney, ditto
Mr. Richard Winstone, ditto
Mr. Joshua Williams, ditto
Mr. William Wiltshire, Bath
Mr. Thomas Williams, of St. Catherines, Memb. of the Stewards Lodge
Mr. Robert Williams, Hatter, Lombard-street
Mr. John Wilton, R. W. M. Chelsea
Mr. Wood-cock, of the Paladian Lodge, Hereford
Mr. James Wood, Hosier, in Abby Church-yard, Bath
Mr. Thomas Woolley, of the Lodge of Perfect Friendship, Bath
Dr. Francis Woodward, P. M. Bristol
Mr. John Wood, Kingston, R. W. M.
Mr. William Worth Tower-street
Mr. Robert Worth, ditto
Mr. Henry Wood, Gunner in the Royal Navy
Mr. John Woollacott, of the Woolpack and White-Hart Lodge
Mr. John Wollacombe, of the Topsham Lodge
Mr. Beauvais Wood, R. W. M. Tiverton
Mr. Ralph Wotton, Attorney at Law, Trentham, Staffordshire, R. P.
Mr. Edward Woodward, Coach-maker, Mary-le-bone
Thomas Wright, Esq;
Mr. Samuel Wright, Haydon-square, Minories
Mr. O. Wright, Nottingham Warehouse, Holbourn
Mr. William Wright, Philpot-lane, W. S. W.
Mr. Christopher Wren, jun. Surgeon
Mr. J. Wyatt, Surgeon, Great Newport-street
Penruddock Wyndham, Esq; Salisbury
Richard Wynne, Esq; Somerset-house Lodge, R. P.
Mr. William Wybrow, St. James's
Colonel Wynard, W. S. W. Chelmsford Lodge

Y

Mr. Samuel Yeatherd, of the Lodge at Crediton
Mr. Morgan Yeatman, Wine Merchant, Dorchester

Mr.

Mr. John Yeomans, Hair-dreſſer, Strand R.W. M.
Mr. Thomas Yeaw, Brewer, Hammerſmith
Mr. Milford Young, Doctor's-Commons
York, the Lodge at, ten Copies

Z

Moſes Zuntz, Eſq; Strand.

The following Names have either been accidentally omitted, *or were* received too late *to be inſerted in their proper Places.*

A

Mr. John Allen, Attorney at Law, Clements-Inn, R.W.M. and P. G. M. for Lancaſhire
Mr. John Aſſey, Surgeon, Taunton

B

Thomas Brown, Eſq; Plas-ſtreet, near Taunton, Somerſetſhire
Mr. Theo. Bell, W. S. W. of the Chequer Lodge, Charing-croſs

C

Captain Cæſar
John Cabbell, M. D. Taunton, P. M. Roy. Paper
Mr. Choyce, Peruke-maker, May's Buildings
Mr. Mat. Clarke, Briſtol
Mr. Francis Cann, Park-lane, R. W. M.
Mr. Church, Attorney at Law, Ledbury
Capt. Arch. Campbell, of the Marines

D

Mr. Thomas Dyne, GRAND SWORD BEARER
William Dixton, Eſq; Taunton, Somerſetſhire

F

Mr. Fricker, Grocer, Taunton

H

Mr. Wm. Henry, of the Craven Arms, Carnaby-market
John William Holwell, Eſq; four Copies, Royal Paper

Mr.

M

Mr. Henry May, Distiller, W. S.W. of Greenwich

N

Mr. Thomas Newcomen, Merchant, at Taunton

ERRATA.

Litteral Mistakes, or Inaccuracies in pointing, if such there be, the Reader will have the Candour to pass over; but as the *following Errata* affect the Sense, he will be pleased to correct *them* with his Pen.

Page 10, line 19, for *satisfying*, read *gratifying*.
16, l. 3, read *evert*.
18, l. 2, read *Parent*.
19, l. 13, for *of*, read *to*.
24, l. 2, read *entitled*.
27, last Line but one, read *delivered him*.
38, last Line but one, read *Government*.
68, l. 16, for *and if*, read *if such*.

INTRODUCTION.

IF we duly consider MAN, we shall find him a *social* being; and in effect, such is his nature, that he cannot well subsist alone: For out of *society* he could neither preserve life, display or perfect his faculties and talents, nor attain any real or solid happiness.

Had not the GOD of Nature intended him for society, he would never have formed him subject to such a variety of wants and infirmities. This would have been highly inconsistent with divine wisdom, or the regularity of omniscience: on the contrary, the very necessities of human nature unite men togethet, and fix them in a state of mutual dependence on one another. For select the most perfect and accomplished of the human race, a HERCULES or a SAMPSON, a BACON or a BOYLE, a LOCKE or a NEWTON, nay, we need not except SOLOMON himſelf, and ſuppoſe him fixed alone, even in this happy country, where nature, from her bounteous ſtores, ſeems to have formed another *Eden*, and we ſhould ſoon find him deplorably wretched; and by being deſtitute of a ſocial intercourſe, deprived of every ſhadow of happineſs.

Therefore, for the eſtabliſhment of our felicity, providence in its general ſyſtem with regard to the government of this world, has ordained a reciprocal connexion between all the various parts of it, which cannot ſubſiſt without a mutual dependence; and from the human ſpecies, down to the loweſt parts of the creation, one chain unites all nature. This is excellently obſerved, and beautifully deſcribed, by a late celebrated poet, in the following lines.

God in the nature *of each being founds*
Its proper *bliſs, and ſets its* proper *bounds*;
But as he form'd a whole, *the* whole *to bleſs*,
On mutual wants *built mutual happineſs*.
So from the firſt eternal order *ran*,
And creature link'd to creature, man to man.

POPE.

Under theſe circumſtances, men muſt of neceſſity form aſſociations for their comfort and defence, as well as for their very exiſtence.

Had

Had revelation been altogether ſilent in this point, yet we might by the mere light of nature have eaſily diſcovered it to be our duty to be *kindly affectioned one to another.* No ſyſtem can be more agreeable to the common ſentiments of mankind, nothing built upon ſurer terms of equity and reaſon, than that I ſhould treat my fellow-creature with the ſame candour and benevolence, with the ſame affection and ſincerity I ſhould expect myſelf. It is true this was not delivered in expreſs words till the time of *Moſes*, nor ſo fully explained and underſtood as at the coming of the prophets. Yet we have great reaſon to believe that it was the firſt law revealed to *Adam*, immediately upon his fall, and was a genuine precept of uncorrupted human nature. That every one is naturally an enemy to his neighbour, was the malevolent aſſertion of a late *philoſopher* [HOBBS:] one who vainly thinking himſelf deeper verſed in the principles of man than any before him, and having miſerably corrupted his own mind by many wild extravagancies, concluded, from ſuch acquired corruption, that all men were naturally the ſame. How to reconcile a tenet of this kind with the juſtice and goodneſs of a ſupreme being, ſeems a taſk too difficult for the moſt knowing perſon to execute; and what the author himſelf was contented barely to lay down, without the leaſt ſhew of argument in its defence. That God ſhould be a being of infinite juſtice, creating us in a *neceſſary* ſtate of *dependance* on, and at the ſame time bring us into the world with inclinations of enmity and cruelty towards each other, is a contradiction ſo palpable, as no man can aſſert conſiſtently with a reverential notion of his maker. And were there no ſufficient proofs againſt it, even from our imperfect ideas of the creator, the very laws of nature would confute it.

By the law of nature, I would be underſtood to mean, that will of God which is diſcoverable to us by the light of reaſon without the aſſiſtance of revelation. Now nothing is more evident than this grand maxim, That whatever principles and actions have an inſeparable connection with the public happineſs, and are neceſſary to the well-being of ſociety; are fundamental laws of nature, and bear the ſtamp of divine authority.

This will more evidently appear from the following conſideration: When the GRAND ARCHITECT OF THE UNIVERSE had, with the greateſt wiſdom and moſt exact proportion, formed this globe, and repleniſhed it with every thing neceſſary for life and ornament, he laſt of all created *man*, after his own image, enduing him with rational and immortal powers, adequate to the preſent and future happineſs for which he was deſigned.

But though he found himſelf in paradiſe where every thing abounded for his ſuſtenance and delight,

light, yet for want of a creature of the ſame rational nature with himſelf, his felicity was incompleat; ſo much did the innate ideas of ſociety poſſeſs and influence the human mind from its firſt exiſtence, that the higheſt enjoyments without participation, were taſteleſs and unaffecting *; a ſtrong proof that even in the original ſtate of human nature, ſelfiſh and narrow principles had no ſhare; and that to communicate bleſſings was to increaſe them. To gratify his wiſhes, enlarge his mind, and eſtabliſh his (before imperfect) happineſs, God created an help meet for him, "*Woman*, his *laſt beſt* gift;" thereby enabling him to exchange the ſolitary for the *ſocial* life; an imperfect for a perfect bliſs! Now the human mind began to expand; a new train of ideas and affections ſucceeded; its joys were increaſed, and its wiſhes accompliſhed. Theſe diſpoſitions were continued with the ſpecies, and *man* has ever ſince had recourſe to *ſociety* as an eſſential means to humanize his heart and meliorate the enjoyments of life.

But, alas! he being created *free* in the exertion of the faculties, both of body and mind,

---

* Our grandſire *Adam*, e'er of *Eve* poſſeſt,
Alone, and e'en in Paradice unbleſt,
With mournful look the bliſsful ſcene ſurvey'd
And wander'd in the ſolitary ſhade;
The Maker ſaw, took pity, and beſtow'd
Woman, the laſt, the beſt reſerve of GOD!

and theſe faculties being vitiated by ſin in our firſt parents, the taint became hereditary, and ſoon broke out in ſymptoms which foreboded deſtruction to the peace and happineſs of the world. *Cain* furniſhed an early and terrible inſtance of the truth of this aſſertion, when of the firſt two brothers that ever were on earth, one fell a victim to the envious fury of the other, and demonſtrated that a train of new paſſions had taken poſſeſſion of the human heart. *Envy*, *hatred*, and *revenge* now made their appearance, and *bloodſhed* and *diſcord* followed. Ties of *conſanguinity* firſt cemented mankind; but after the ſons of *Noah* had rendered the earth more populous, and the confuſion of languages had ſeparated one family from another, vice and impiety boldly reared their heads. Therefore to remedy theſe dreadful evils, and avert their conſequences, the uniting various men and different orders, in the bands of friendſhip, ſeemed the beſt and ſureſt method; and was indeed the greateſt and moſt effectual defence againſt the univerſal depravity of corrupted human nature: It was *here* alone protection could be had, from the attacks of violence, or the inſinuations of fraud, from the force of brutal ſtrength or the ſnares of guilty deſign.

Further to promote theſe ends, and ſecure ſuch bleſſings, *laws* were now neceſſarily introduced for the ſafety and advantage of every individual; and of their good effect *we* in this

nation

nation ought to be better judges than the whole world besides, for *ours*, we may extol, as *St. Paul* expresses himself, " in confidence of boasting."

If we confine ourselves to *particular* parts of society, and treat on bodies of men, who, though members of, and subordinate to the general system, unite themselves into distinct communities, for their own immediate advantage, and relatively for the public benefit, we shall find some entering into such associations upon different views, and to answer various purposes. We, of this nation in particular fear no enemy at our gates, no violence from our neighbours, and I hope no treachery from our friends; but assemble with men of similar opinions and manners, not out of necessity for the preservation of our lives, but to render them more beneficial to others and pleasing to ourselves; by enabling us to perform those duties, and afford that assistance to each other in a *united* capacity, which as *individuals* we were unable to do.

To this kind of associations, I shall confine myself in the following work; and shall treat on the ancient institution of *free and accepted Masons* in particular; an establishment founded on the benevolent intentions of extending and confirming mutual happiness, upon the best and truest principles of *moral* and *social* virtue.

For

For among many inſtances of the above truth, apparent to every intelligent perſon, let us reflect, that in all ſocieties and governments there are ſome indigent and miſerable, whom *we* are taught to regard as objects of our compaſſion and our bounty; it is our indiſpenſable duty, to aid ſuch with our council, commiſerate their afflictions, and relieve them in their diſtreſs.

'Tis what the happy to th' unhappy owe,
For what man gives, the gods on him beſtow.

POPE.

This principle is the *bond of peace*, and the *cement of maſonic affection.* Free Maſons eſteem it as a virtue of the moſt diffuſive nature, not to be confined to particular perſons, but extended to the whole human race, to adminiſter aſſiſtance to whom, is their higheſt pride and their utmoſt wiſh, eſtabliſhing friendſhips and forming connexions, not by receiving, but conferring benefits. As ſoon might the builder *alone* work through each tedious courſe of an edifice without the aſſiſtance of his fellow-crafts-men, as poor *helpleſs unaſſiſted* man, toil through each chequered ſtage of human life.

The Almighty has therefore furniſhed men with different capacities, and bleſſed them with various powers, that they may be mutually beneficial and ſerviceable to each other; and

indeed

indeed wherever we turn our eyes and thoughts, we ſhall find ſcope ſufficient to employ thoſe capacities, and exerciſe thoſe powers, agreeable to the celebrated maxim of the great *Socratic* diſciple, *that we are not born for ourſelves alone.*

That we may not be too much elevated with the contemplation of our own abundance, we ſhould *conſider*, no man comes into this world without *imperfections*; that we may not decline being ſerviceable to our fellow-creatures, we ſhould *reflect*, that all have their portion for *improvement*; that we may not be remiſs or reluctant in good offices, we ſhould *remind* ourſelves, however affluent our fortune, we are not entirely *independent of others*, and where much is given, much will be required: we are commanded to be *fruitful* in good works; and throughout the whole creation we ſhall find no precedent for inutility or indolence, for he that contributes neither ſtudy, labour, or fortune to the public, is a deſerter of the community. All human affections, if directed by the governing principle of reaſon, tend to promote ſome uſeful purpoſe. *Compaſſion*, if properly exerted, is the moſt beneficient of all human virtues, extending itſelf to a greater number of objects, exciting more laſting degrees of happineſs, than any other. *Some* affections are indeed more fierce and violent, but *their* action, like a ſudden exploſion of combuſtibles, is no ſooner begun than its force is ſpent.

The rational, the manly pleaſure, which neceſſarily accompanies *compaſſion*, can only be known to thoſe who have experienced its effects; for who ever relieved the indigent, and did not at the ſame time receive the higheſt gratification? to ſee a fellow-creature labouring in agony and pain, or ſtruggling under the oppreſſive burthen of helpleſsneſs and want, preſently raiſes pity in the human breaſt, induces us to ſympathize with the object in his diſtreſs, and inſpires us with the tender diſpoſitions of *charity* and aſſiſtance.

If our pleaſure was to be eſtimated in proportion to its extent and duration, that of doing good muſt rival and outſhine all others the mind is ſuſceptible of, being both from its nature, and the variety of objects on which it acts, greatly ſuperior to the fleeting and unſatisfactory enjoyment ariſing from the ſatisfying our ſenſual appetites. Hence *compaſſion*, both on account of its duration, from its pleaſing effects, and its unbounded utility to the world, ought to be highly valued and duly cultivated by all who conſult their own felicity, or the proſperity and intereſt of that country or people to which they belong.

It would be abſurd to dwell longer on this head, as I am addreſſing a body who in every age, from the earlieſt times to this preſent day, have been juſtly celebrated for their diſintereſted liberality, and whoſe proceedings have been con-

conſtantly directed by the deſires of doing good, to, and promoting the happineſs of every individual.

From the foregoing conſiderations, the neceſſity of conſtituting particular ſocieties, is ſtrikingly obvious: for next to the veneration of the ſupreme Being, the love of mankind ſeems to be the moſt promiſing ſource of real ſatisfaction: It is a never-failing one to him, who, poſſeſt of this principle, enjoys alſo the means of indulging it; and who makes the ſuperiority of his fortune, his knowledge, or his power, ſubſervient to the wants of his fellow-creatures. It is true, there are few whoſe abilities or fortunes are ſo adapted to the neceſſities and infirmities of human nature, as to render them capable of performing *works* of *univerſal beneficence*, but a *ſpirit* of *univerſal benevolence* may be exerciſed by all; and the bounteous Father of nature has not proportioned the pleaſure to the greatneſs of the *effect*, but to the greatneſs of the *cauſe*. Here let not my meaning be miſtaken; I would not be underſtood, to inſinuate that we are ſo obliged to be bountiful that *nothing* will excuſe us; for it is an univerſal maxim among *maſons*, that, "*Juſtice muſt precede charity*;" and except where the exigencies of the diſtreſſed call for IMMEDIATE relief, we ſhould always recollect our *natural connections* and *debts to the world*, whenever our diſpoſitions may prompt us to beſtow any *ſingular* bounty. And give me leave to obſerve, it is not the idle,

in-

indolent or extravagant, but the induſtrious, tho' diſtreſſed brother, who has a juſt title to our extraordinary beneficence; a circumſtance that ought always to direct the exertion of the above virtue.

Having thus in ſome meaſure, deduced the nature and neceſſity of *ſociety*, and in part ſhewn the duties incumbent upon us as members of it, May we as upright men and maſons faithfully diſcharge the duties of our various ſtations; and above all, be ever ready to do to others as we could in their circumſtances reaſonably wiſh to be done unto.

They who move in a higher ſphere, have indeed a larger province wherein to do good; but thoſe of an inferior degree will be as eminently diſtinguiſhed in the manſions of bliſs, (if they move *regularly*, if they are *uſeful* members of ſociety) as the higheſt. He who performs his part beſt, not he who perſonates an exalted character, will meet with applauſe. For the *moon*, though it borrows its light from the *ſun*, alſo ſets forth the glory of God; and the flowers of the field declare a providence equally with the ſtars of the firmament.

To conclude then, let me exhort all my worthy brethren to be diligent in the cultivation of every *moral* and *ſocial* virtue, for ſo long only do we act conſiſtently with the principles of our venerable inſtitution. Then what has been ſaid, though on an occaſion far more important to mankind, may not improperly be appropriated as the badge of our reſpectable order, "By this ſhall all men know that you belong to the *brethren* if your hearts glow with affection, (not to *maſons* alone but) to the whole race of mankind." And well indeed may *ours* be called a happy inſtitution! whoſe ſupreme wiſh is founded on the trueſt ſource of felicity, and whoſe warmeſt endeavours are ever exerted in cementing the ties of human nature by acts of benevolence, charity and ſocial affection: and who, amidſt the corruption and immorality of the latter ages, have maintained in their aſſemblies the genuine principles and unſullied reputation acquired and eſtabliſhed in the firſt.

Whilſt qualities like theſe direct your proceedings and influence your actions, *Free Maſonry* muſt ever be revered and cultivated, by the juſt, the good, and the exalted mind, as the ſureſt means of eſtabliſhing *peace, harmony, and good will amongſt men.*

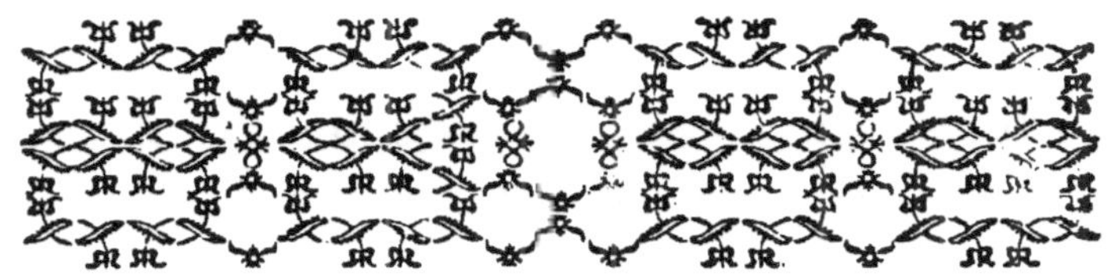

A

DISQUISITION,

&c. &c. &c.

THE antiquity and utility of FREE-MASONRY, being generally acknowledged in moſt parts of the habitable globe, it would be as abſurd to conceive it required new aids for its ſupport, as for him who has the uſe of ſight to demand a proof of the *riſing* and *ſetting* of the ſun. Nevertheleſs, in compliance with the requeſts of many worthy brethren, I ſhall lay before my readers ſome

ſtrictures

ſtrictures on the *origin*, *nature* and *deſign* of that INSTITUTION; and with prudent reſerve confute and avert the many ſhameful and idle falſehoods which are induſtriouſly propagated by its enemies, the better to inform the candid and well meaning, who might not readily know how to inveſtigate the truth, or want leiſure and opportunity for that purpoſe.

With this view I have made it my buſineſs to collect a great number of paſſages from writers eminent for their learning and probity, where I thought they might ſerve to illuſtrate my ſubject. The propriety of ſuch proceeding is too obvious to need any apology.

If our firſt parent and his offsping had continued in the terreſtrial paradiſe, they would have had no occaſion for mechanic arts, or any of the ſciences now in uſe; ADAM being created with all thoſe perfections and bleſſings, which could either add to his dignity, or be conducive to his real welfare: In that happy period he had no propenſity to evil, no perverſeneſs in his heart, no darkneſs or obſcurity in his underſtanding; for had he laboured under theſe maladies he would not have been a *perfect man*, nor would there be any difference betwixt man in a ſtate of innocence, and in a ſtate of degeneracy and corruption. It was therefore in conſequence of his wilful tranſgreſſion that any evils came upon him. And having loſt his innocence, he in that dreadful moment forfeited likewiſe his ſuper-

natural

natural lights and infused knowledge, whereby every ſcience (as far as human nature is capable of) was rendered *familiar* to him without the tedious labour of ratiocination, requiſite to men even of the greateſt abilities, whoſe ideas after all, remain weak and imperfect.

From this remarkable and fatal *æra*, we date the *neceſſity* and *orign* of the *ſciences*. Firſt aroſe *divinity*, whereby was pointed out to fallen man the ways and will of God, the omnipotence and mercy of an offended creator: Then *law**, as directing us to diſtribute juſtice to our neighbour, and relieve thoſe who are oppreſſed or ſuffer wrong. The *royal art* was beyond all doubt coeval with the *above* ſciences, and was carefully handed down by *Methuſelah*, who dyed but a few days before the *General Deluge*, and who had lived 245 years with ADAM, by whom

* No ſooner had ADAM tranſgreſſed the divine command, than we find him cited to appear before the *Almighty Judge*. When, ſelf-accuſed, after hearing his defence, ſentence was pronounced upon him; a method of proceeding in *that* ſcience, which has been adopted in criminal caſes, by the more enlightened nations from that period and example down to the preſent day.

he

he was inſtructed in all the myſteries of this ſublime *Science*, which he faithfullycommunicated to his *Grandſon* NOAH, who tranſmitted it to *Poſterity*. And it has ever been preſerved with a veneration and prudence ſuitable to its great importance, being always confined to the knowledge of the *worthy* only. This is confirmed by many inſtances, which men of reading and ſpeculation (eſpecially ſuch as are of *this ſociety*) cannot ſuffer to eſcape them.

At *firſt* mankind adhered to the leſſons of *nature*; ſhe uſed neceſſity for the means, urged them to invention, and aſſiſted them in the operation. Our primitive fathers ſeeing the natural face of the earth was not ſufficient for the ſuſtenance of the animal creation, had recourſe to their faithful *tutoreſs*, who taught them how to give it an artificial face, by erecting habitations and cultivating the Ground; and theſe operations among other valuable Effects, led them to ſearch into and contemplate upon the nature and properties of *lines*, *figures*, *ſuperfices* and *ſolids*; and by *degrees*, to form the *ſciences* of *geometry* and *architecture*, which have been of the greateſt utility to the *human* ſpecies. Hence we were firſt taught the means whereby we might attain *practice*, and by practice introduce ſpeculation.

*

From the *flood* to the days of king *Solomon*, the *liberal arts* and *ſciences* gradually ſpread themſelves over different parts of the globe; every nation having had ſome ſhare in their propagation; but according to their different manners, ſome have cultivated them with more accuracy, perſeverance and ſucceſs than others; and though the *ſecrets* of the *royal art*, have not been *indiſcriminately* revealed, they have nevertheleſs been communicated in every age to ſuch as were worthy to receive them.

But I am not at liberty to undraw the curtain, and publicly diſcant on this head: It is *ſacred*, and ever will remain ſo; thoſe who are honoured with the truſt, will not *reveal* it except to the truly qualified brother, and they who are ignorant of it cannot *betray* it.

I ſhall however obſerve, that *this art* was called *royal*, not only becauſe it was originally practiſed by *kings* ‡ and *princes*, who were the

---

‡ The celebrated SELDEN tells us, that civil ſociety, beginning firſt in particular families, under œconomick rule, repreſenting what is now a common-wealth, had in its ſtate, the huſband, father, and maſter, as *king*, (SELDEN's works, tom. 3, col. 927.) And in ABRAHAM's treaty, with the ſons of HETH, for a burying place for SARAH, they ſtile him a *mighty prince*; as indeed he was. (*Gen.* xxiii. *v.* 6.) In a word, not only *Adam*, but all the ſucceeding patriarchs, as well before as after the *flood*, had by the law of nature *kingly* power over their reſpective families.

first professors of it, but likewise on account of the superiority which so sublime a science gave its disciples, over the rest of mankind.

This supreme and divine knowledge being derived from the ALMIGHTY CREATOR to ADAM, its principles ever since have been and still are, most sacredly preserved and inviolably concealed. For as all things in process of time are liable to decay and corruption, the ancient professors wisely foreseeing the great abuses which their exalted mysteries might sustain, if *generally* made known, determined to confine the knowledge of them only to *select* brethren, men whom they had found by long experience to be well versed in the *general* principles of the society, and who were eminent for their piety, learning and abilities.

Hence it is that a man may be sufficiently able to acquit himself in every *test* that is laid down by our present *institution*, to prove his regular initiation therein, and also to shew that he is not unacquainted with its *general* principles, and *yet* at the same time he may be totally ignorant and undeserving of the more valuable parts of the *ancient society*. These, like the aduta of the ancient temples, are hid from vulgar eyes. It is not every one who is barely initiated into *Free-Masonry*, that is entrusted with all the great mysteries thereto belonging: They are not attainable as things of course, nor by every capacity; for as Mr. LOCKE very justly observes, (speaking

ſpeaking of this *ſociety*) "Though *all* have a right and opportunity (*if they be worthy and able to learn*) to know *all* the *arts* and *myſteries* belonging to it, yet that is not the caſe, as ſome want capacity and others induſtry to acquire them." Nevertheleſs, ſuch is the real felicity, neceſſarily reſulting from a knowledge and practice of the *general* principles of this *fraternity*, as *alone* was ever found ſufficient to intitle it to a preference of all other human inſtitutions.

From the *earlieſt* ages of antiquity, the *royal art* was ever taught with the greateſt *circumſpection*, not in ſchools or academies to a promiſcuous audience, but was confined to certain families; the rulers of which inſtructed their children or diſciples, and by this means conveyed their *myſterious* knowledge to poſterity.

After the *flood*, the profeſſors of this art (according to *ancient* traditions,) were firſt diſtinguiſhed by the name of *Noachidæ*, (or ſons of NOAH) afterwards by that of *ſages* or *wiſe men*, (men inſtructed as MOSES in all the wiſdom of the *Egyptians*,) *Chaldeans*, *philoſophers*, *maſters in Iſrael*, &c. and were ever venerated as *ſacred* perſons. They conſiſted of perſons of the brighteſt parts and genius, who exerted their utmoſt abilities in diſcovering and inveſtigating the various myſteries of nature, from whence to draw improvements and inventions of the moſt uſeful conſequences. Men, whoſe talents were

not

not only employed in ſpeculation, or in private acts of beneficence; but who were alſo public bleſſings to the age and country in which they lived, poſſeſſed with moderate deſires, who knew to conquer their paſſions; practiſers and teachers of the pureſt morality, and ever exerting themſelves to promote the harmony and felicity of *ſociety*. They were therefore conſulted from all parts, and venerated with that ſincere homage which is never paid but to real merit, and the greateſt and wiſeſt potentates on earth, eſteemed it an addition to their imperial dignities, of be enrolled among ſuch bright ornaments of human nature.

A principal excellence which rendered them famous among men, was *Taciturnity*, which in a peculiar manner *they* practiſed and inculcated as neceſſary for concealing from the *unworthy*, what few were qualified to learn, and ſtill fewer to teach.

In the firſt ages of the world, *ſcience* was in a low ſtate; becauſe the uncultivated manners of our *forefathers* rendered them *in general* incapable of that knowledge which their *poſterity* have ſo *amply* enjoyed: the profeſſors of the *royal art*, therefore, found it abſolutely requiſite, to exclude the more unworthy and barbarous part of mankind from their aſſemblies, and to conceal their

their myſteries under ſuch * *hieroglyphicks*, *ſymbols*, *allegory* and *figures*, as *they alone* could explain, (even at *this* day it is indiſpenſible in *us*, to prevent future bad conſequences, by concealing from vulgar eyes the means uſed by them to unfold ſuch myſteries) wherefore the greateſt caution was ever obſerved at *their* meetings, that no *unqualified* perſon might enter amongſt them; and every method was employed to *tyle* them *ſecurely*, and conceal the real intent and deſign of their convocations.

In order to render their proceedings more edifying and extenſively uſeful, *charges* were delivered at *certain* times, as well for regulating the conduct of the fraternity, as preſerving that

---

* *Hieroglyphics* are properly emblems or ſigns of divine, ſacred or ſupernatural things, by which they are diſtinguiſhed from common *ſymbols*, which are ſigns of ſenſible or natural things. HERMES TRISMEGISTUS is commonly eſteemed the inventor of *hieroglyphicks*; he firſt introduced them into the heathen theology, from whence they have been tranſplanted into the Jewiſh and Chriſtian.

Sacred things, ſays HIPPOCRATES, ſhould only be communicated to ſacred perſons. Hence it was, that the ancient *Egyptians* communicated to none but their kings and prieſts, and thoſe who were to ſucceed to the prieſthood and the crown, the ſecrets of nature and the myſteries of their morality and hiſtory; and this they did by a kind of *Caballa*, which, at the ſame time that it inſtructed them, only amuſed the reſt of the people. Hence the uſe of *hieroglyphicks*, or *myſtick* figures, to veil their morality, politics, *&c.* from profane eyes. SPON.

mark

mark of diſtinction, which their *ſuperior* merit juſtly entitle them to.

Several of thoſe *ancient orations* are ſtill extant, by which it appears, that among others, one of their principles was to *inculcate* by *precept*, and *inforce* by *example*, a ſtrict obſervance of the *moral* law, as the chief means of ſupporting government and authority. And it is evident that they thereby effected their purpoſe, and ſecured to themſelves the favour, reſpect, and eſteem of the world in general; and, notwithſtanding the indolence and ignorance of ſome ages, the various countries, languages, ſects, and parties, through which *maſonry* has paſſed, always ſubjected to the neceſſity of *oral* tradition, and under the numerous diſadvantages with which the *maſters* of the *royal art* had to ſtruggle in the courſe of many *centuries*, ſtill does it retain, in a great degree, its original perfection:— a circumſtance that not only bears honourable teſtimony of intrinſick worth, but is highly to the praiſe of thoſe to whom this *important truſt* has been from time to time committed.

After this *conciſe* and *general* account of the *ancient profeſſors* of the *royal art*, and the ſublime truths which *they* were poſſeſſed of, and were by them tranſmitted down to poſterity in the manner before deſcribed, we will proceed to the building of that glorious edifice, at which period this *ſociety* became a *regular* and uniform *inſtitution*, under the denomination

mination of *Free and accepted Maſons*, whoſe cuſtoms and proceedings I ſhall deſcribe, as far as may be *neceſſary* and *prudent*.

Though the *almighty* and *eternal* JEHOVAH has no occaſion for a temple, or houſe to dwell in, for the *heaven of heavens* is not capable of containing his immenſity, yet it was his divine will, that a *tabernacle* ſhould be erected for him in the wilderneſs by MOSES, and afterwards a *temple*, by SOLOMON, at *Jeruſalem*, as his ſanctuary; both of which were to be conſtructed, not according to human invention, but after a *pattern* which the *Lord* himſelf had given. The *whole model* of the *tabernacle* was ſhewn to MOSES on mount *Sinai*; (*Exod.* xxv. ver. 9.) and the *pattern* of the *temple* was likewiſe given to DAVID by the hand of the *Lord*, and by him delivered to SOLOMON his ſon (1 *Chron.* xxviii. ver. 11.)

The *tabernacle* might be conſidered as the *palace of the moſt High*, the *dwelling of the God of Iſrael*; wherein the *Iſraelites*, during their journeyings in the wilderneſs, performed the chief of their religious exerciſes, offered their ſacrifices, and worſhipped *God* *. It was *thirty* cubits in length, *ten* in breadth, and *ten* in height; it was divided into *two* partitions, the *firſt* was called *the Holy Place*, which was *twenty* cubits long and *ten* wide: *here* were placed *the table of*

---

* The tabernacle was erected about A. L. 2513.

ſhew-bread, *the golden candleſtick*, and *the golden altar of incenſe*. The *ſecond* was called *the moſt holy place*, whoſe length was ten cubits, and breadth ten cubits, wherein, before the building of the *temple*, the ark of the covenant was kept, which was a ſymbol of God's gracious preſence with the *Jewiſh* church. *The moſt holy place* was divided from *the holy place* by a curtain or veil of very rich cloth, which hung upon *four pillars* of *Shittim wood*, that were covered with *plates of gold*. (*Exod.* xxvi. ver. 31. *Heb.* ix. ver. 23.)

The *temple* erected by SOLOMON (which was built after the *model* of the *tabernacle*) at *Jeruſalem*, had its foundation laid in the year of the world 2992, before CHRIST 1008, before the vulgar æra 1012; and it was finiſhed A. L. 3000, and dedicated 3001, before CHRIST 999, before the vulgar æra 1003. The *glory* of this temple did not conſiſt in the magnitude of its dimenſions; for though it was twice as long and capacious every way as the *tabernacle*, yet, alone, it was but a ſmall pile of building. The main grandeur and excellency were in its *ornaments*: the workmanſhip being every where exceeding curious, and the overlayings prodigious: in its *materials*, being built of new large ſtones, hewn out in the moſt curious and ingenious manner; in its *out-buildings*, which were large, beautiful and ſumptuous:—but, ſtill more admirable in this majeſtic edifice, were thoſe extraordinary marks of divine favour with which it was honoured,

noured, viz. *The ark of the covenant*, in which were put the *tables of the law*, and the *mercy ſeat*, which was upon it; from whence the divine oracles were given out, with an audible voice, as often as *God* was conſulted in behalf of his people; the *Schechinah*, or the *divine preſence*, manifeſted by a viſible cloud reſting over the mercy ſeat; the *urim* and *thummim*, by which the high-prieſt conſulted GOD in difficult and momentous caſes, relating to the public intereſt of the nation; the *holy fire*, which came down from heaven, upon the altar, at the conſecration:---*theſe* indeed were excellencies and beauties derived from a divine ſource, diſtinguiſhing and exalting this ſacred ſtructure above all others. (1 *Kings* xviii. ver. 38.) *David*, filled with the hopes of building this *temple*, declared his intentions to NATHAN the prophet; (2 *Sam.* vii. ver. 1, 2, 3.) but this was not permitted him, becauſe his reign had been attended with wars, bloodſhed and ſlaughter, and he ſtill had to contend with many powerful enemies; but, though forbid to execute this divine and glorious work, he made conſiderable preparations for that purpoſe; which having done, and drawing towards his latter end, he aſſembled all the princes and chief perſons of his kingdom, and ordered and encouraged SOLOMON publicly, and in their preſence, to purſue ſuch his intention, (1 *Chron.* xxviii. ver. 1---10.) and delivered the *pattern*, or *ſcheme*, of all the houſes, &c.

(ver. 11, 12.) the courſes of the *prieſts* and *levites*, (ver. 11---31) and likewiſe the *pattern* of the *cherubims*, (ver. 18.) earneſtly exhorting his *ſervants*, in regard to the tender age of his ſon, SOLOMON, who was yet but very young, to yield him their councils and aſſiſtance, in erecting a palace, not deſigned for man, but for the LORD GOD. DAVID himſelf gave towards the building of the temple, out of his own treaſures, beſides a vaſt variety of precious ſtones, *three thouſand* talents of gold of *Ophir*, and *ſeven thouſand* talents of ſilver. (1 *Chron.* xxix. ver. 25.)

The *princes* of his kingdom followed the glorious example of their king, and gave *five thouſand* talents and *ten thouſand* drachms of gold, *ten thouſand* talents of ſilver, *eighteen thouſand* talents of braſs, and *one hundred thouſand* talents of iron, as alſo a great many of the moſt precious ſtones. (1 *Chron.* xxix. 6, 7, 8.

When DAVID the king was dead *; and SOLOMON was eſtabliſhed on his throne, he reſolved to carry into execution his father's deſign, and to erect a *temple* to his great Creator.

For which purpoſe he applied to HIRAM king of *Tyre*, for aſſiſtance; and having readily obtained a promiſe of what he deſired, and procured from thence, and other parts, men and ma-

* A. L. 2989.

terials

terials sufficient for his intentions, he began that great and majestic fabrick; and as method and order are known and confessed to be essentials requisite in conducting all great designs and undertakings, he proceeded in the following manner. He numbered and classed his men according to their skill and abilities, viz.

1. *Harodim*, princes, rulers or provosts, in number - - - - -	300
2. *Menatzchim*, overseers and comforters of the people in working, that were expert *master-masons* -	3300
3. *Ghiblim*, stone-squarers, polishers and sculptors; and *Ishchotzeb*, men of hewing; *Benai*, setters, layers or builders, being able and ingenious fellow-crafts - - - - -	80,000
4. The levy out of *Israel*, appointed to work in *Lebanon* one month in three, 10,000 each month, under the direction of noble *Adoniram*, who was the junior grand warden -	30,000
Whole number employed, exclusive of the two *grand wardens*, and of the men of burthen, who were the remains of the old *Canaanites*, who being *bondmen*, are not numbered among *masons*, was - - -	113,600

SOLOMON likewise partitioned the *fellow-crafts* into certain *lodges*, appointing to each, one to preside

preſide *as a maſter*, aſſiſted by two others *as guardians*, that they might receive commands in * a regular manner, take care of the tools and jewels, and be duly paid, fed, cloathed, &c.

Theſe neceſſary regulations being previouſly ſettled, to preſerve that *order and harmony* which would be abſolutely requiſite among ſo great a number of men, in executing ſo large a work: He alſo took into conſideration, the *future* agreement and proſperity of the craft, and deliberated on the beſt means to ſecure them by a laſting cement.

Now, *brotherly love* and *immutable* fidelity, preſented themſelves to his mind, as the moſt proper *baſis* for an *inſtitution*, whoſe aim and end ſhould be to eſtabliſh permanent unity among its members, and to render them a ſociety, who, while *they* enjoyed the moſt perfect felicity, would be of conſiderable utility to *mankind*. And being deſirous to tranſmit it under the ancient reſtrictions as a bleſſing to future ages, SOLOMON decreed, that whenever they ſhould aſſemble in their lodges to diſcourſe upon, and improve themſelves in the *arts and ſciences*; and whatever elſe ſhould be deemed proper topics to encreaſe their knowledge, they ſhould likewiſe inſtruct each other in *ſecrecy* and *prudence*, morality and

---

* Vide. Book of Conſtitutions, P. 21.

good-

good fellow-ſhip; and for theſe purpoſes he *eſtabliſhed* certain *peculiar* rules and cuſtoms to be invariably obſerved in their converſations, that their minds might be enriched by a perfect acquaintance with, and practice of, every *moral*, *ſocial* and *religious duty*, *leſt* while they were ſo highly honoured by being employed in raiſing a *temple* to the great JEHOVAH, they ſhould neglect to ſecure to themſelves an happy admittance into the *celeſtial* lodge, of which the temple was only to be a *type*.

Thus did our wiſe *grand maſter* contrive a plan by *mechanical* and *practical alluſions*, to inſtruct the *craftſmen* in principles of the moſt *ſublime ſpeculative philoſophy*, tending to the glory of GOD, and to ſecure to *them* temporal bleſſings *here*, and eternal life *hereafter*; as well as to unite the *ſpeculative* and *operative* maſons, thereby forming a two-fold advantage from the principles of *Geometry* and *Architecture*, on the one part, and the precepts of wiſdom and ethicks on the other. The *next* circumſtance which demanded SOLOMON's attention was, the readieſt and moſt effectual method of paying the wages of ſo vaſt a body of men, according to their reſpective degrees, without error or confuſion, that nothing might be found among the maſons of *Sion*, ſave harmony and peace. ‡ *This* was ſettled in a manner well known

‡ *Kings* 6,7.

to all regularly made maſons, and therefore is unneceſſary, as alſo *improper*, to be mentioned here.

Theſe arrangements being adjuſted, the noble ſtructure was began ‡ and conducted with ſuch grandeur, order and concord, as afforded SOLOMON the moſt exalted ſatisfaction, and filled him with the ſtrongeſt aſſurance, that the *royal art* would be further encouraged in future ages, and amongſt various nations, from the exellencies of this temple, and the fame and ſkill of the Iſraelites, in the beauty and ſymmetry of architecture therein diſplayed.

He was likewiſe ſenſible, that when this building ſhould be *compleated*, the craftſmen would diſperſe themſelves over the whole earth; and being deſirous to *perpetuate* in the moſt effectual manner, the *harmony* and *good-fellowſhip* already eſtabliſhed among them, and to ſecure to *themſelves*, their *future* pupils, and their *ſucceſſors*, the honour and reſpect due to men whoſe abilities were ſo great, and would be ſo juſtly renowned: In conjunction with HIRAM king

‡ This noble ſtructure was erected in mount *Moriah*, in the month *Zif*, which anſwers to our *April*, being the ſecond month of the ſacred year (A. L. 2992.) and was carried on with ſuch prodigious expedition, that it was compleatly finiſhed in little more than *ſeven years*, in the month *Bul*, which anſwers to our *October*. A. L. 2999, and was dedicated the year following.

of

of *Tyre* and *Hiram Abiff*, the deputy grand maſter, concerted a proper plan to accompliſh his intentions; in which it was determined, that, in conformity to the practice of the original profeſſors of the *royal art*, general diſtinguiſhing *characteriſticks* ſhould be eſtabliſhed for a proof of their having been fellow labourers in this glorious work, to deſcend to their ſucceſſors in all future ages, who ſhould be in a *peculiar* manner qualified to cultivate the ſublime principles of this noble eſtabliſhment; and ſuch were adopted and received accordingly. With reſpect to the METHOD which would be *hereafter* neceſſary for *propagating* the principles of the ſociety, SOLOMON *purſued* the uniform and *ancient* cuſtom, in regard to *degrees of probation* and *injunctions* to *ſecrecy*; which he himſelf had been obliged to comply with before he gained a perfection in the *royal art*, or even arrived at the ſummit of the *ſciences*; therefore, tho' there were no *apprentices* employed in the building of the *temple*; yet as the *craftſmen* were all intended to be promoted to the degree of *maſters*, after its dedication; and as *theſe* would ſecure a ſucceſſion, by receiving *apprentices* who *might* themſelves in *due* time alſo become *maſter maſons*, it was determined, that the *gradations* in the ſcience ſhould conſiſt of *three* diſtinct *degrees*, to *each* of which ſhould be adapted a particular diſtinguiſhing teſt, which *teſt*, together with

 the

the *explication*, was accordingly ſettled and communicated to the *fraternity*, previous to their diſperſion, under a neceſſary and ſolemn injunction to ſecrecy: and they have been moſt cautiouſly preſerved, and tranſmitted down to poſterity by *faithful* brethren, ever ſince their emigration. Thus the *center of union* among *free-maſons*, was firmly fixed; their *cabala* regulated and eſtabliſhed; and their principles directed to the excellent purpoſes of their original intention.

CHAP. II.

THE harmony and connexion of the society of *free-masons*, and the excellent precepts and principles thereof, have produced the utmost good consequence, not only to the particular members of it, but frequently to the nations where it has been cultivated and practised.

For united by the endearing name of *brother*, they live in an affection and friendship, rarely to be met with even among those whom the ties of consanguinity ought to bind in the firmest manner. That intimate union which does so much honour to humanity in general, in the particular intercourse, which prevails among *free-masons*, diffuses pleasure that no other institution can boast. For the name which they mutually use one towards another, is not a vain compliment, or an idle parade; no, they enjoy in common, all the felicities of a true brotherhood. Here, merit and ability ſecure to their poſſeſſors, an honourable regard, and a reſpectful diſtinction, which every one receives with an unaffected complacency and a perfect humility; conſtantly exerting himſelf for the general good, without vanity, and without fear. For they who are not adorned with the ſame advantages, are neither mortified nor jealous. No one contends for ſuperiority; here emulation is only with a view to pleaſe; the man of ſhining abilities, and thoſe unbleſſed with ſuch ornaments, are here equally admitted; all may here perform their parts; and what may ſeem ſurprizing amongſt ſuch a variety of characters, haughtineſs or ſervility, never appear. The greateſt admit of a ſocial familiarity; the inferior is elevated and inſtructed, conſtantly maintaining by *theſe* means a beneficent equality.

With reſpect to the converſation which they hold during their aſſemblies, it is conducted with the moſt perfect decency: here it is an univerſal maxim, never to ſpeak of the abſent but with reſpect; ill-natured ſatire is excluded; all raillery is forbidden; they will not even ſuffer the leaſt irony, or the poignant ſtrokes of wit, becauſe they generally have a malignant tendency; they *tolerate* nothing which carries with it even the *appearance* of vice.

Their pleaſures are never imbittered by ungrateful reflections, but produce a ſerene and laſting compoſure of mind. They flow not like a torrent which deſcends with noiſe and impetuoſity, but like a peaceful ſtream within its own channel, ſtrong without violence, and gentle without dulneſs.

This exact regularity, very far from occaſioning a melancholly ſerioufneſs, diffuſes, on the contrary, over the heart, and over the underſtanding, the moſt pure delights; the bright effects of enjoyment and hilarity ſhine forth in the countenance; and altho' the appearances are ſometimes a little more ſprightly than ordinary, *decency* never runs any riſque; 'tis *wiſdom* in *good-humour*. For if a brother ſhould happen to forget himſelf, or in his diſcourſe ſhould have the weakneſs to uſe ſuch expreſſions as are diſtinguiſhed under the name of *liberties*, a formidable *ſign* would immediately call him to his duty; a *brother* may miſtake as a *man*, but he hath opportunity and courage to recover himſelf, becauſe he is a *free-maſon*. Altho' order and decorum are always ſcrupulouſly obſerved in the lodges of *free-maſons*; *theſe* exclude not in any wiſe gaiety and chearful enjoyment: The converſation is animated, and the kind and brotherly cordiality that preſides there, affords the moſt pleaſing ſenſation.

Theſe particulars may juſtly recall to our minds the happy time of the divine *Aſtrea!* when there was neither ſuperiority nor ſubordination, becauſe men were as yet untainted by vice, and uncorrupt.

Having

Having now given a *general* ſketch of the nature of this *inſtitution*, from whence a *candid* reader may form no inconſiderable idea of that compoſed wiſdom, and laudable harmony which governs in the fellowſhip of *free-maſons*; we ſhall proceed in taking ſome notice of the ſeveral accuſations frequently brought againſt it.

And *firſt*; As none can venerate and eſteem the *fair-ſex*, more than *free-maſons* do, we cannot but reckon it a misfortune that the *ladies* ſhould be offended at their non-admiſſion into this *order*; and the more ſo, as they no ſooner learn with what moderation the maſons comport themſelves in their aſſemblies, but without knowing the reaſon why they are not admitted, they cenſure us with all the ſeverity their delicate minds are capable of. This we muſt beg leave to ſay, is intirely owing to miſtaken *prejudice*, for a little reflection would convince them, that their not being received in *this* inſtitution, is not in the leaſt ſingular. They ſtand in the ſame predicament with reſpect to the *prieſthood*, and many other *particular* ſocieties; the *ſolemn* aſſemblies of the ancients, the *ſenates* of Pagan, and the *conclaves* of papal Rome, all *national* ſenates and *eccleſiaſtical* ſynods, *univerſities* and *ſeminaries* of learning, &c. &c. with which they might with equal propriety be offended.

Next to the diſpleaſure of the ladies, we will conſider a charge with regard to *governments*, which in *other* countries, *leſs* happy in their con-

ſtitution

ſtitution than *our own*, has at different times been unjuſtly proſecuted againſt this fraternity.

It has been imagined, that there is every thing to be feared for the tranquillity of the ſtate, from a numerous aſſociation of men of merit and character, intimately united under the ſeal of *ſecrecy*. I agree that this ſuſpicion has in it ſomething very ſpecious; for if the paſſion of a ſingle man, hath cauſed (as we have ſeen more than once) ſtrange revolutions in a ſtate; what might not be produced by a body ſo numerous and united, as that of free and accepted maſons; were they liable to theſe intrigues and cabals, which pride and ambition inſtill but too often into the human heart.

But there is nothing to be apprehended from *free-maſons* in theſe reſpects; they are actuated by the love of order and peace, and are as much attached to *civil* ſociety, as united among themſelves; 'tis in this ſchool, that a man may learn moſt effectually, what reſpect, what ſubmiſſion, what veneration he ought to have, for his God, his country and his king; 'tis among *them*, that ſubordination is fully practiſed and deemed a virtue, not a yoke.

Equally without reaſon, have they alſo been accuſed of holding aſſemblies for no other purpoſe, than that of ſpeaking with the greater freedom on *religious*, as well as *political* matters. Theſe topics are never ſuffered to be agitated; for it is a fundamental maxim of this inſtitution,

inſtitution, to prohibit all ſuch diſputes. The God of heaven, and the rulers of the earth, are by them inviolably reſpected. And with regard to the ſacred perſon of *majeſty*, every congregated lodge, ſolemnizes the name with all poſſible grandeur and reſpect.

Thus theſe accuſations fall to the ground.

It is alſo alledged by the objectors to *free-maſonry*, that upon the *initiation* of a member into this myſtery, he lays himſelf under a ſolemn obligation by an oath, with very ſevere penalties. This by them is pronounced an unwarrantable proceeding. Certainly theſe perſons are as ignorant as they are ungenerous, and for want of better judgments form erroneous notions, and from falſe premiſes draw falſe concluſions. To obviate *this* objection, we will trace the antiquity of ſwearing, and obſerve the different cuſtoms adopted by the ancients on this head; afterwards examining the *nature* of an oath, ſuppoſing (for the ſake of argument, but not granting) that one is required as ſet forth by the adverſaries of maſonry; we will conſider how far, it is, or is not, warrantable in the preſent caſe.

We are informed by *ſacred* hiſtory, what was the cuſtom of *ſwearing* among the *Hebrews*, who ſometimes ſwore by *ſtretching forth their hands* (as in. Gen. xiv. v. 27.) ſometimes the party ſwearing *put his hand under the other's thigh*. (Gen. xxiv. v. 21. xlvii. v. 29. which was the

manner

manner of adminiſtration uſed by ABRAHAM and JACOB. Sometimes * *ſtanding before the altar*, as we read in *Kings*; which was alſo the cuſtom of the *Athenians*(1), the *Carthaginians*(2), and the *Romans*(3).

The *Jews* chiefly ſwore by *Jeruſalem*, by the *temple*, by *the gold of the temple*, by *the altar*, and *the gift on the* altar.

The *Greeks* eſteemed it an *honour* paid *their* DEITIES, to uſe their names in ſolemn contracts, promiſes and aſſeverations; and call them to witneſs mens truth and honeſty, or to puniſh their falſehood and treachery. This was reputed a ſort of religious adoration, being an acknowledgment of the *omnipotence* and *omnipreſence*, and by conſequence of the *divinity* of the Being thus invoked: and the *inſpired* writers, for the ſame reaſon, forbid to ſwear by the *Pagan* DEITIES, and commanded to ſwear by the *true* GOD. Thus in *Deuteromony* (chap. vi. v. 15) *thou ſhalt fear the Lord thy God, and ſerve him, and ſhalt ſwear by his name.* And in *Jeremiah* (chap. v. v. 7.) *How ſhall I pardon thee for this? thy children have forſaken me, and ſworn by them that are no Gods*; and to forbear other

---

* *Kings*, viii. 31.—(1) Alex. ab. Alex. L. 5. c. 10.—(2) *Livius*, Dec. 3. l. 1.—(3) *Juven.* Sat. 3. *Val. Max.* L. 9. c. 3.

instances,

inſtances, the worſhippers of the *true* God, are by DAVID, repreſented to ſwear by him, *i. e.* by invoking his name.

The *antiquity* of ſwearing, as well as the *manner* of adminiſtring an oath, having now been ſufficiently ſhewn; we will in the next place, as far as may be neceſſary, take notice of the fundamental principles of this eſtabliſhment, as the propereſt method to form a right judgment of it; and then in anſwer to the preſent objection, we will examine how far an *oath* would, or would not be juſtifiable, on the initiation of a maſon, and *ſuppoſing* it to be required even under ſuch pænal ſanctions as have been pretended.

If we examine the *laws* and *regulations* of *free-maſonry*, it will appear that the *end* and *purport* of it is truly laudable, being calculated to regulate our paſſions, to aſſiſt us in acquiring knowledge of the arts and ſciences, and to promote morality and beneficence, as well as to render converſation agreeable, innocent, and inſtructive; and ſo to influence our practice, as to make us uſeful to others, and happy in ourſelves. With regard to the relation we have (as members) to ſociety in general, it will appear equally evident from the ſaid regulations, that a *free-maſon* is to be a peaceable ſubject, conforming cheerfully to the government under which he lives, is to pay a due deference to his

his ſuperiors; and from his inferiors is to receive honour rather with reluctance than to extort it. He muſt be a man of univerſal benevolence and charity, not tenacious of his abundance, when the exigences of his fellow creatures lay the juſteſt claim to his bounty.

Maſons not only challenge, but have ever *ſupported* that character amongſt the *honeſt* and *candid* part of mankind, whoſe equity and reaſon would never ſuffer them to entertain ill-grounded prejudices.

The great Mr. LOCKE appears to have been ſo delighted with ſome of our principles, that he tells Lady MASHAM (to whom he was writing on this ſubject) "that it was his wiſh, they were communicated to *all* mankind, ſince there is nothing more true than what the maſons teach; that the better men are, the more they love one another: *virtue* having in itſelf ſomething ſo amiable as to charm the heart of all who behold it*."

And *another* ‡, ſpeaking of *free-maſons*, ſays, "no abuſe is tolerated among them, no intemperance allowed; modeſty, union and humility,

* The manuſcript from which this and a ſubſequent quotation are made, is printed in the appendix to this diſquiſition.

‡ Vid. Rel. Caſt. vol. 6. fol.

are ſtrongly recommended." Again, "this ſociety is no ways offenſive to religion, good manners or political government; it has and does ſtill flouriſh in Great Britain and its dominions under the protection of the greateſt perſonages, even *princes* of the royal blood."

Mr. CHAMBERS in his *Cyclopædia*, alſo teſtifies, "that *free* and *accepted maſons*, are a very ancient ſociety, or body of men, ſo called either from ſome extraordinary knowledge of maſonry or building, which they were ſuppoſed to be maſters of, or becauſe the firſt founders of this ſociety were of that profeſſion."

"They are very conſiderable, both for number and character; being found in ever country in Europe, and conſiſting principally of perſons of merit and conſideration. As to antiquity, they lay claim to a ſtanding of ſome thouſand years, and 'tis ſaid, can trace up their original as early as the building of *Solomon's temple*."

"What the end of their inſtitution is, ſeems ſtill to be a ſecret, tho' as much of it as is known, appears laudable, as it tends to promote friendſhip, ſociety, mutual aſſiſtance and good fellowſhip."

"The brethren of this family, are ſaid to be poſſeſſed of a number of *ſecrets*, which have been religiouſly obſerved from age to age. Be their other good qualities whatever they will, it

is

is plain they are mafters of *one*, in a very great degree, namely SECRECY."

Now let us afk, if a number of perfons have formed themfelves into a body with a defign to improve in ufeful knowledge, to promote univerfal benevolence, and to cultivate the focial virtues of human life, and have bound themfelves by the folemn obligation of an oath, to conform to the rules of fuch inftitution, where can be the impiety, immorality or folly of fuch proceeding? Is it not the cuftom of moft communities; in the ftate, amongft the learned bodies, in commerce, &c. a cafe too commonly known to require a recital of particular inftances. I fhall therefore content myfelf with adding this obfervation, viz. That bifhop SAUNDERSON, an eminent cafuift, in his lectures on the fubject of oaths, very judicioufly afferts, that when a thing is not by any precept or interdict human or divine, fo determined, but every man may at his choice do, or not do, as he fees expedient, let him do what he will, he finneth not. (1 *Chron.* chap. vii. v. 36.) As if CAIUS fhould fwear to fell his land to TITIUS, or to lend him an hundred crowns, the anfwer is brief, an oath in this cafe, is both lawful and binding. (*Prælect.* 3 *Sect.* 15.)

And as the principles of this inftitution are truly praife-worthy, containing thofe valuable requifites which will ever fecure the efteem and admiration of all *good men*, (as well as moſt aſſuredly the envy of the *bad*,) we will put this plain queſtion; is not the deſign of it of equal importance to the publick, with the lending of an hundred crowns to a private man? the anſwer and the conſequences are both evident: that an *oath* on the ſubject of *free-maſonry*, if required, is both lawful and obligatory.

As for the terror of a penalty; it is a miſtaken notion to imagine that the *ſolemnity* of an oath, adds any thing to the *obligation*: or that the oath is not equally binding without *any* penalty at all.

I ſhall add a few more quotations from the ſame excellent *caſuiſt*, and leave the *explanation* and *application* to the intelligent.

A *ſolemn* oath of itſelf, and in its own nature, is not more obligatory than a *ſimple* one; becauſe the obligation of an *oath*, ariſeth preciſely from *this*, that God is invoked as a witneſs and avenger, *no leſs* in the *ſimple* one, than in the *ſolemn* and *corporal*; for the *invocation* is made preciſely by the *pronounciation of the words* (which is the ſame both in the ſimple and ſolemn) and not by any *corporal motion* or *concomitant ſign* in which the *ſolemnity* of the *oath conſiſts*. Prælect. 5. Sect. 12.

And it is a matter well worthy the conſideration of every man, that as the object of a lawful oath, is God alone, ſo it contains a ſolemn

ſolemn confeſſion of his *omnipreſence*, that he is with us in every place; of his *omniſcience*, that he knoweth all *ſecrets* of the heart, that he is a *maintainer of truth* and *an avenger of falſehood*: of his juſtice, that he is willing, and of his *omnipotence*, that he is *able* to puniſh thoſe that by *diſregard to their oaths*, ſhall diſhonour him.

It is therefore of a very dangerous tendency for perſons who have once *taken* an *oath*, to trifle and play with the *force* of it, even ſuppoſing the *occaſion* of ſuch obligation was actually of ſmall moment in itſelf. And this is poſitively determined by the ſame writer, in the following words, and ought to be a caution to *all*, not to violate an oath, leſt they incur the fatal conſequences of *real perjury*.

" A *voluntary* oath is the more binding for being *voluntary*, becauſe there is no ſtricter obligation than that we take *willingly* on ourſelves." (Prælect. 4. Sect. 11.) And in another place he is more particular, where a matter is ſo *trivial*, that it is not worth the deliberation of a wiſe man, nor ſignifies a ſtraw whether it be done or not done; as to reach up a chip, or to rub one's beard, or for the *ſlightneſs* of it, is not much to be eſteemed, as to give a boy an apple, or to lend a pin; an oath is binding in matters of the *leaſt moment*; becauſe *weighty* and *trivial things* have a like reſpect unto *truth* and *falſehood*; and further, becauſe every party *ſwearing*, is bound to perform *all* he *promiſed*, as far as he is able, and as far it is *lawful:* to give an apple to a boy, is both poſſible and lawful, he is bound therefore to perform it: He ought to fulfil his oath." (Prælect. 3. Sect. 15.)

This is likewiſe confirmed by Moses, (*Numb.* xxx. v. 2.) "If a man ſwear an oath to bind his ſoul with a bond, he ſhall not break his word; he ſhall do according to all that proceedeth out of his mouth." And (*Zeck. chap.* v.) It is threatened that every one that ſweareth falſely, ſhall be cut off by the *curſe:* "I will bring *it* forth, ſaid the Lord *of* Hosts, and it ſhall enter into the houſe of *him the ſweareth falſely by my name*; and it ſhall remain in the midſt of his houſe, and ſhall conſume it, with the timber thereof, and the ſtones thereof."

The *objectors* being thus anſwered with reſpect to the *lawfulneſs* of an oath, ſuppoſing one to be required on the initiation of a *free-maſon* (as to the *certainty* of which conjecture is their only ſupport) I ſhall next take notice of the charge brought againſt them on account of *ſecrecy*; one of their grand characteriſticks; and the innocent cauſe of all the perſecutions and reproaches they ſuffer.

We are condemned for keeping the eſſentials of our inſtitution from the knowledge of thoſe who are not members of it: Which, 'tis ſaid,

* muſt

must sufficiently prove them to be of a bad nature and tendency, else why are they not made publick for the satisfaction of mankind.

If *secrecy* be a virtue, (a thing never yet denied) can that be imputed to us as a *crime*, which has been considered an excellence in all ages? Does not SOLOMON, the wisest of men, tell us, *He that discovers secrets is a traitor, but a man of a faithful spirit concealeth the matter.*

In conducting all worldly affairs, *secrecy* is not only essential, but absolutely necessary; and was ever esteemed a quality of the greatest worth.

Thus we find the great FENELON makes ULYSSES, in the system of the education which he delivers to his friends for his son TELEMACHUS, particularly enjoin them above all, to render him just, beneficient, sincere, and faithful in *keeping secrets*; a precept that afterwards produced the best of consequences to the young prince, of whom it is recorded, that with this great excellence of taciturnity, he not only divested himself of that close mysterious air, so common to the reserved, but also constantly avoided telling the least untruth in support of this part of his character. A conduct! highly worthy the imitation of every one to whom secrets are intrusted, affording them a pattern of openness, ease and sincerity; for while he seemed to carry his whole heart upon his lips, communicating what was of no importance, yet he knew how to stop just in the proper moment, without proceeding to thoſe things which might raiſe any ſuſpicion, or furniſh even a hint to diſcover the purpoſes of his mind.

If we turn our eyes back to antiquity, we ſhall find the old *Egyptians* had ſo great a regard for *ſilence* and *ſecrecy* in the myſteries of their religion, that they ſet up the God *Harpocrates* (vid. *imagines deorum a vincentio chartario*) to whom they paid peculiar *honour* and *veneration*, who was repreſented with his *right hand placed near the heart, and the left down by his ſide*, covered with a ſkin before, full of eyes and ears, to ſignify, that of many things to be ſeen and heard, few are to be publiſhed.

And among the ſame people, the great goddeſs *Iſis*, the *Minerva* of the *Greeks*, had always an image of a *Sphynx* placed at the entrance of her temples, to denote that ſecrets were there preſerved under ſacred coverings, that they might be kept from the knowledge of the *vulgar*, as much as the riddles of that creature.

Jamblicus, in his life of Pythagoras, confirms the above opinion, by obſerving, that from the myſterious knowledge of the *Egyptians*, that philoſopher drew the ſyſtem of *his* ſymbolical learning and inſtructive tenets, ſeeing that the principles and wiſe doctrines of this nation, were ever kept *ſecret* among themſelves, and were delivered down, not in writing, but only by oral tradition. And indeed ſo cautious and prudent were they in theſe matters, that every

diſciple

disciple admitted to their wise and scientific mysteries, was bound in the most *solemn* manner to conceal such mysteries from the vulgar, or those whose ideas were not sufficiently exalted to receive them. As a proof of this, we need only recollect the story of *Hipparchus*, a *Pythagorean*, who having out of spleen and resentment, violated and broke thro' the several engagements of the society, was held in the utmost detestation, expelled the school as one most infamous and abandoned, and as he was dead to the principles of virtue and philosophy, had a tomb erected for him, according to their custom, as though he had been naturally dead. The shame and disgrace that justly attended so great a breach of truth and fidelity, drove the unhappy wretch to such despair, that he proved his own executioner; and so abhorred was even his memory, that he was denied the rites and ceremonies of burial used to the dead in those times; instead of which, his body was suffered to lie upon the shore of the Isle of *Samos*.

Among the *Greek* nations, the *Athenians* had a statue of brass, which they awfully revered; this figure was without a tongue; by which *secrecy* was intimated.

The *Romans* had a goddess of silence, named ANGERONA, represented with her fore finger on her lips, a symbol of *prudence* and *taciturnity*.

ANNAXARCHUS, who (according to PLINY) was apprehended in order to extort his *secrets* from

from him, bit his tongue in the midſt, and afterwards ſpit it in the tyrant's face, rather chuſing to loſe that organ, than to diſcover thoſe things which he had promiſed to conceal.

We read likewiſe that CATO the *Cenſor*, often ſaid to his friends, of three things which he had good reaſon to repent, the principal was *divulging a ſecret*.

The *Druids* in our own nation (who were the only prieſts among the ancient *Britons*) committed nothing to writing. And CÆSAR obſerves that they had a *head* or *chief*, who exerciſed a ſort of excommunication, attended with dreadful *penalties* on thoſe, who either *publiſhed* or *prophaned* their myſteries.

Therefore, ſince it evidently appears from the foregoing inſtances (among many other) that there ever were *ſecrets* amongſt mankind, as well reſpecting *ſocieties* as *individuals*, and that the keeping thoſe *inviolable*, was always reputed an indiſpenſable duty, and attended with an honourable eſtimation; It muſt be very difficult to aſſign a ſufficient reaſon why the ſame practice ſhould be at all wondered at, or leſs approved in the *free and accepted maſons* of the preſent age, than they were among the wiſeſt men, and greateſt philoſophers of antiquity.

The general practice and conſtant applauſe of the *ancients*, as well as the cuſtoms of the *moderns*, one would naturally imagine ſhould be ſufficient to juſtify *maſons* againſt any charge

of

of ſingularity or innovation on this account; for how can this be thought ſingular, or new, by any one who will but calmly allow himſelf the ſmalleſt time for reflection.

Do not all incorporated bodies amongſt *us*, enjoy this liberty without impeachment or cenſure? an *apprentice* is bound to keep the ſecrets of his maſter; a *freeman* is obliged to conſult the intereſt of his company, and not proſtitute in common the myſteries of his profeſſion; ſecret *committees* and privy *councils*, are ſolemnly enjoined not to publiſh abroad their debates and reſolutions. In *courts martial*, the members are bound to *ſecrecy*; and in many caſes for more effectual ſecurity an *oath* is adminiſtred.

As in *ſociety* in *general*, we are united together by our *indigencies* and *infirmities*, and a vaſt variety of circumſtances contributing to our mutual and neceſſary dependence on each other, (which lays a grand foundation for terreſtrial happineſs, by ſecuring general amity and the reciprocation of good offices in the world) ſo, in all *particular ſocieties*, of what ever denomination, they are all conjoined by a ſort of cement; by *bonds* and *laws* that are peculiar to each of them, from the higheſt aſſemblies to the loweſt. Conſequently the injunctions of *ſecrecy* among *free-maſons*, can be no more unwarrantable than in the *ſocieties* and *caſes* already pointed out: and to *report*, or even to *inſinuate*, that they are, muſt argue a want of *candour*, a want

of

of *reaſon*, and a want of *charity.* For by the laws of nature, and of nations, every *individual*, and every *ſociety*, has a right to be ſuppoſed *innocent* 'till *proved* otherwiſe.

Yet notwithſtanding the *myſteries* of our profeſſion are kept inviolable, none are excluded from a full knowledge of them, in *due* time and manner, upon *proper* application, and being *found* capable and worthy of the truſt. To form *other* deſigns and expectations, is building on a a ſandy foundation, and will only ſerve to teſtify, that like a raſh man, their diſcretion is always out of the way when they have moſt occaſion to make uſe of it.

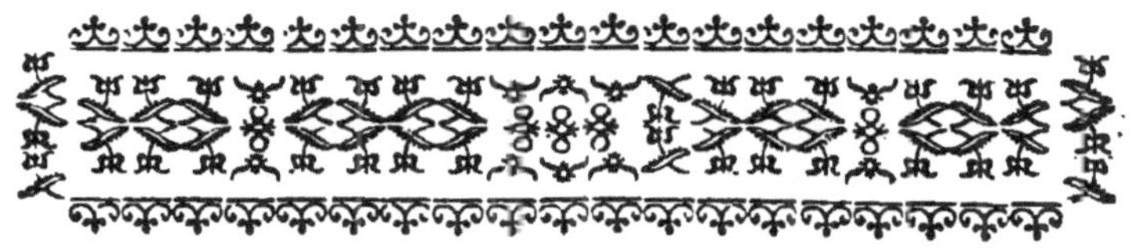

CHAP. III.

E will now proceed to the next objection, viz. That "*masonry* is a *trifling* institution, and that our principles contain nothing valuable in them."

These *censurers* finding it easier to decry a science than to understand it, are with wicked endeavours attempting to depreciate that which they cannot attain to, and would make their *necessity* appear a virtue, and their *ignorance* the effect of choice.

This turn of mind is the despicable offspring of *envy*, and so selfish are such men, that they would rather prefer having the whole circle of the arts and sciences abolished, was it in their power, than that others should be possessed of a knowledge, which they are themselves totally *unacquainted* with and *undeserving* of.

But alas! they disquiet themselves in vain; *we* who *are* masons, cannot but laugh at and pity such feeble attacks, and are heartily sorry for those

thoſe who have no better underſtandings than to regard them.

Did they *know* any thing of our *profeſſion*, they could not but eſteem it, for they would be convinced that it is founded on the moſt exalted principles of *morality* and *ſocial virtue*; tending to promote the true happineſs of mankind in general, the peace and ſatisfaction of every individual in particular; to cenſure then and vilify what they are entirely ignorant of, diſcovers the baſeneſs of their diſpoſitions, and how little they are qualified to paſs their judgments in matters of ſuch importance. Therefore, though we commiſerate their defects, we muſt at the ſame time be allowed to pronounce them *unworthy* our further notice.

Had our *inſtitution* contained nothing commendable or valuable in it, 'tis impoſſible it ſhould have exiſted, and been patronized by the wiſe, the good and great, in all ages of the world. For we cannot ſuppoſe that men, diſtinguiſhed by every accompliſhment that can adorn human nature, would embrace or continue in principles which they found to be nugatory, erroneous or contemptible. Therefore the advice which GAMALIEL (*Acts.* v. ver. 38.) wiſely gave to *the perſecutors* of the *apoſtles*, might with great propriety be recommended to theſe *railers* againſt *free-maſons*. They may aſſure themſelves, that if there was no more in our inſtitution than their *little* minds ſuggeſt, it

would

would have fallen to the ground ages paſt, but the contrary being the caſe, they may ſafely conclude, it will continue to exiſt notwithſtanding any oppoſition, for ages yet to come.

Perhaps it will be ſaid, that the *moral* and *ſocial* principles *we* profeſs, are equally neceſſary to the ſupport of *every* well regulated ſociety; how then came *maſons* to appropriate the merit of ſuch principles to themſelves? I anſwer, they are not only deemed neceſſary, but *taught*, and brought into *practice* in the *lodge*; they are familiarized to us by ſuch a plain, pleaſing and peculiar method, that they ſeem no longer leſſons or rules, but become inherent principles in the breaſt of every *free-maſon*. But from the corrupt ſtate and diſpoſition of mankind, there are ſome who will *always* make it their buſineſs to aſperſe and ridicule whatever they ſuſpect has the leaſt beauty or excellency in it.

Theſe *envious beings*, having juſt ſenſe enough to imagine, that *ſcandal* is eaſier hit off than *praiſe*; and that *ſatyr* will ſooner procure them a name than *panegyrick*, and looking at *all* ſocieties through falſe and narrow mediums, they form judgments of *them* from their trifling *ſelves*; acting in direct contradiction to the *apoſtles* exhortation to the *Philippians*, "If there be any virtue, if there be any praiſe, they will *condemn* thoſe things," notwithſtanding the ſtrength of reaſon with which they are accompanied; notwithſtanding the apparent benefit and advantage they may bring to mankind; ſo little reliſh have *they* for things *excellent* in themſelves, ſo inattentive are *they* to the force of the cleareſt reaſoning, and ſo enveloped in *ignorance* and prejudice, that nothing is ſufficient to *convince* them. I don't mean that *ignorance* which implies a *want* of knowledge*, but that affected and preſumptuous *folly* which *deſpiſes* it. And of ſuch SOLOMON ſays, "ſeeſt thou a man that deſpiſeth inſtruction? there is more hope of a *fool* than of him."

If therefore theſe *accuſers* have any remains of modeſty, if the *aſſertors* of ſuch calumny *can* ever bluſh, they are now put to the trial; for whilſt they deal thus freely with the principles and proceedings of perſons of the greateſt honour and diſtinction, they are only diſcovering to the *judicious* part of mankind, the weakneſs of their heads and the wickedneſs of their hearts. How truely do they come under the ſtandard of that deſcription which JUSTUS LIPSIUS, an eminent writer, has given us of this *abominable* ſect.

---

* The natural and proper effect of a bare want of knowledge is, that men forbear to paſs *any* judgment, upon what they underſtand *not*; and that they neither contend *for*, nor *againſt* any thing, before they have *ſome reaſon* to determine them ſo to do.

Calumny,

" *Calumny*, ſays he, is a filthy and pernicious infection of the tongue; generally aimed by the *moſt wicked and abandoned* part of mankind, againſt the *moſt worthy* and *deſerving* of eſteem, and wounds them unexpectedly. And to whom is it pleaſing? To the *moſt vile*, the *perfidious*, the *talkative*. But what is its ſource? From what origin does it proceed? from *falſehood*, as it's father; from *envy*, as its mother; and from *curioſity*, as its nurſe?"

Would ſuch perſons exerciſe but a very ſmall portion of reaſon and reflection, they would readily perceive the madneſs of their attempt to depreciate a ſociety which has ever withſtood and repelled every attack made againſt it; ſtill acquiring additional honour and ſtrength; ſuch proceedings affecting it no more, than a javelin thrown by the feeble hand of old age, that never reaches, or at moſt makes no impreſſion on its deſtined mark.

CHAP. IV.

THE last accusation brought against *free and accepted masons*, which I shall take any notice of, is, that they make use of *hyeroglyphic* figures, *parabolical* and *symbolical customs* and *ceremonies*, *secret words* and *signs*, with different *degrees* of *probation* peculiar to themselves: these are also censured.

What *evil* these *refined* casuists can point out in *such* proceedings, is not easy to imagine. But I think it no very difficult undertaking to *justify* them against any objection.

It is well known that *such* customs and ceremonies, are as ancient as the first ages of the world, the philosophers of which practised the method of inculcating their *sublime truths* and *important points of knowledge* by *allegory* and *mythology*, the better to secure them from descend-

ing

ing into the familiar reach of every inattentive and unprepared novice, from whom they might not meet with the veneration they deserved, and therefore become too *familiar*, and *contemptible*; for which reason they were accustomed to proceed with the utmost care and prudence. And ORIGEN tells us, (*Origen Contra Celsum*) " The *Egyptian* philosophers had *sublime notions* which they kept *secret*, and never discovered to the people, but under the vail of *fables* and *allegories*; also other eastern nations concealed *secret mysteries* under their religious ceremonies, a custom *still* retained by many of them.

An interpretation therefore of these *allegories*, &c. as they come under my notice, shallbe attended to; and will, I flatter myself, exactly square with the present purpose.

Of all the *symbols* appropriated to JUPITER, I shall only mention the *crown of rays*, with the *petasus* and *caduceus*, with which he is represented. The *first* denotes the *power* of the supreme being; the *other*, that *power* ought to be accompanied with *prudence*.

The *cock* was a symbol peculiar to MERCURY, as expressive of that vigilance which was so very necessary to him, destined to execute many functions; as sometimes this *emblem* hath an ear of corn in his bill, it may serve to point out to man, that plenty and happiness will be the consequence of *care* and *attention*.

The

The *club* is the ſymbol of HERCULES, and denotes *ſtrength.*

The various ſymbols belonging to the goddeſs DIANA, were *Oxen*, *Lyons*, *Griffins*, *Stags*, *Sphynx's*, *Bees*, *Boughs*, *Roſes*, &c. which ſignify in a myſtical ſenſe, the *univerſe*, with all its productions.

The ſtory of MINERVA is entirely *allegorical*, relating, that JUPITER having devoured METIS, (i. e. prudence) conceived MINERVA, and was delivered of her. This *ſymbol* means plainly that *prudence* is wholly in GOD, and that he produces her externally by the wonderful works conſtantly manifeſted in his government of the univerſe.

It will not be foreign to my ſubject, to take notice that cities, rivers, regions, and even the various parts of the globe had their proper *ſymbols*, which were ſo many *enſigns* to *diſtinguiſh* them. *Cities* were ſignified by women with *towers* on their heads: The *eaſt* is repreſented by a woman mounted upon a carr, with *four horſes*, *riſing* as they go. The *weſt* is ſignified likewiſe by a woman in a carr drawn by *two horſes:* The *genius* that precedes her, together with the *horſes falling down*, by which the *weſt*, or ſun *ſetting* is denoted.

The *ſymbol* of ASIA, was a woman with a *mural crown*, holding an *anchor*, to denote that the way thither was to croſs the ſea. AFRICA

was

was reprefented by a woman with an *Elephant's trunk* on her *forehead*. *Thus* were the different parts of the world reprefented under their refpective *fymbols* and *hieroglyphics*.

To improve properly on *thefe* myftical writings, we muft bring them home to ourfelves, by way of application.

Firft in a *phyfical* fenfe; for under the various names of *pagan deities*, are concealed the body and fubftance of *natural philofophy*: Under *allegories*, the poets exprefs the wonderful works of *nature*.

Secondly in an *ethical* fenfe; the fcope or intent of *mythologifts*, was not *fable* but *morality*. Their defign was to inform the underftanding, correct the paffions, and guide the will. Examples are laid down to kindle in the mind a candid emulation, leading thro' the *temple* of *virtue* to the *temple* of *Honour*. They fet off in the fulleft colours, the *beauty* of *virtue* and *deformity* of *vice*.

Thirdly in a *theological* fenfe; for let a fkilful hand modeftly draw afide the vail of *poetry*, and he will plainly difcover the majeftic form of *divinity*. I think it is an affertion of *Tertullian* (who lived in an early age of *chriftianity*) that *many* of the poetical fictions had their *original* from the SCRIPTURES. And PLATO is faid by the beft authorities, to have derived the fublimeft principles of his *philofophy*, from fome

writings

writings of MOSES, which he had met with and ſtudied in the courſe of his travels in *Egypt**. Doubtleſs as the *ancients* before the invention of letters, expreſſed their *conceptions* in *hieroglyphicks*, ſo did the *poets* their *divinity*, in *fables* and *parables*.

We alſo find, that even when they ſet up *ſtones* in order to compoſe any *memorial*, there was ſomething expreſſive either in the *number*, of which the monument conſiſted, or in their *ſhape*, or in the *order* and *figure* in which they were diſpoſed; of the firſt kind were the monuments of *mount Sinai*; (*Exod.* xxiv. ver. 4.) and that at *Gilgal*, erected by JOSHUA, upon the banks of *Jordan*; *they* conſiſted of *twelve* ſtones each, becauſe the people of *Iſrael*, (for whoſe ſake the altar was built, and the ſtreams of Jordan dividing themſelves, thereby opening a miraculous paſſage for the whole nation) were principally claſſed into *twelve* tribes (*Joſh.* iv. v. 8.) the ſame number of ſtones: and for the above reaſon were ſet up in the midſt of the place where the *ark* had reſted. (ib. v. 9.)

---

* Whenever it is aſſerted that the *Pagan* accounts of things were borrowed from Revelation recorded in the hiſtory of *Moſes*, it muſt not be underſtood, that *all* the fables and fictions of the *Heathens* were borrowed from thence, but only that the *truths* which appear amongſt their fables and fictions (when ſtript of their *mythological* diſguiſe) were derived from ſome traditions they had of a *Revelation* recorded in the *ſacred hiſtory*.

Likewiſe

Likewise the famous * *pillars before* SOLOMON's *temple*, were not placed there for ornament *alone*; their signification, use and mystical meanings

---

* As there is a seeming contradiction in the accounts of the *height* of these pillars, it may not be amiss here to reconcile that matter. It is said, *he set them up* IN *the porch of the temple*, (1 *Kings* vii. 21.) and *he made before the house two pillars*. And *he reared up the pillars* BEFORE *the temple*, (2 *Chron*. iii. 15, 17. which expressions taken together sufficiently seem to imply the *pillars* were *before* the temple in its porch. But it is not quite so easy to assign the *height* of them. In one place it is said of SOLOMON, *He cast two pillars of brass*, 18 *cubits high each*. (1 *Kings*, vii. v. 15.) In another we read, *he made two pillars of thirty and five cubits high* (2 *Chron*. iii. v. 15.) This seeming inconsistency between the two sacred historians, may be easily reconciled, but at the same time it serves to prove they did not combine together, or were corrected or amended by each other. To reconcile this seeming inconsistency, let us only suppose the *pedestal* or *basis* of the columns to have been 17 cubits high, this added to the 18 cubits (1 *Kings* vii. v. 16. *Jer*. lii. v. 21.) for the *shaft*, will together make exactly 35 cubits, the number mentioned, (2 *Chron*. iii. v. 15.) lastly taking (1 *Kings* vii. v. 16.) five cubits, being the height of the chapiter, we shall have the true height of the pillars, viz. 40 cubits. It is true, that in another place (2 *Kings* xxv. v. 17.) the height of the chapiter is said to have been 3 *cubits*; but here we apprehend we have the dimensions of the *chapiter* only, strictly so called (*Cohereth*, in the Hebrew, or crowning,) which is expressed to have been three cubits, but then there is left to be understood, *the wreathen work on it round about*, which was *two cubits* more, both which sums added, make that of *five*, the number set down before by the same author.

meanings are ſo well known to the *expert* maſons, that it would be both unneceſſary, as it is *improper* for me to aſſign them here; neither are the reaſons why they were made *hollow* known to any but thoſe who are acquainted with the *arcana* of this ſociety; tho' that circumſtance ſo often occurs in ſcripture.

AND with reſpect to ASSEMBLIES and ESTABLISHMENT among men, *they* ever had *ſigns* and *words*, *ſymbolical cuſtoms* and *ceremonies*, different *degrees* of probation, &c. &c. this manifeſtly appears from all hiſtories both *ſacred* and *profane*.

When the *Iſraelites* marched thro' the wilderneſs, we find that the twelve tribes had between

---

It is ſuppoſed that SOLOMON had reſpect to the *pillar* of the cloud, and the *pillar* of fire, which went before the *Iſraelites*, and conducted them in the wilderneſs; and was the token of the divine providence over them: and thus SOLOMON ſet them up before the temple, hoping and praying that the divine light, and the cloud of GOD's glory, would vouchſafe to enter in there, and that GOD and his providence, would dwell among them in this houſe. The pillar on the right hand, repreſented the pillar of the cloud, and that on the left, the pillar of fire. The name of the former ſignifies, *he will eſtabliſh*, which intimates GOD's promiſe to eſtabliſh the throne of *David*, and his people *Iſrael*. The name of the latter ſignifies, *herein is ſtrength*; either alluding to the divine promiſe, in which was all their ſtrength and ſettlement; or rather, to the *ark*, which was within the temple, and called *the ſtrength of the Lord*, (2 *Chron.* chap. vi. ver. 42.)

them,

them, *four* principal banners or ſtandards: every one of which had its particular *motto*: and each ſtandard alſo had a diſtinct *ſign* deſcribed upon it. They encamped round about the tabernacle, and on the *eaſt* ſide were three tribes under the ſtandard of *Judah*; on the *weſt* were three tribes under the ſtandard of *Ephraim*; on the *ſouth* were three tribes under the ſtandard of *Reuben*; and on the *north* were three tribes under the ſtandard of *Dan*; (*Num.* 2d.) and the *ſtandard* of *Judah* was a lion, *that* of *Ephraim* an ox, *that* of *Reuben* a man, and *that* of *Dan* an eagle. Whence were framed the hieroglyphicks of *Cherubims* and *Seraphims*, to repreſent the people of ISRAEL*.

The ancient *prophets*, when they would deſcribe things *emphatically*, did not only draw *parables* from things which offered themſelves, as from the rent of a garment, 1 *Sam.* xv. from the ſabbatic year, *Iſa.* xxxvii. from the veſſels of a potter, *Jer.* xviii, &c. but alſo when ſuch fit objects were *wanting*, they ſupplied them by *their own actions*, as by rending a garment, 1 *Kings* xi. by ſhooting, 2 *Kings* xiii. by making bare their body, *Iſa.* xx. by impoſing ſignificant names *to their*

---

* *A Cherubim* had *one* body with four faces; the faces of a *Lion*, an *Ox*, a *Man*, and an *Eagle*, looking to the four winds of heaven, without turning about, as in *Ezekiel's* viſion, Chap. 1. And the four *ſeraphims* had the ſame four faces with *four* bodies, one face to each body.

ſons, *Iſa.* viii. *Hoſ.* i. hiding a girdle in the bank of *Euphrates*, *Jer.* xiii. by breaking a potter's veſſel, *Jer.* xix. by putting on fetters and yokes. *Jer.* xxvii. by binding a book to a ſtone, and caſting them both into *Euphrates*, *Jer.* li. by beſieging a painted city, *Ezek.* iv. by dividing hair into three parts, *Ezek.* v. by making a chain, *Ezek.* vii. by carrying out houſehold ſtuff, like a captive and trembling, *Ezek.* xii. &c. by which kind of types the *prophets* of old were accuſtomed to expreſs themſelves.

Thus having in an ample manner ſet forth the *antiquity*, *meaning* and *propriety of the uſe* of *hyeroglyphics*, *ſymbols*, *allegory*, &c. from the *earlieſt times*, and among the *wiſeſt and beſt of men*, and if ſuch cuſtoms have been retained by this *ancient. and venerable inſtitution*, ſtrange indeed, and deſtitute of reaſon and juſtice muſt they appear, who ſhould make the leaſt objection to ſuch proceedings; ſuch *miſtaken cenſurers* ſhould be left to the enjoyment of their own *ignorance*, *malevolence* and *detraction*.

The book of *Judges* informs us, that the *Gileadites*, made uſe of an expreſſive and diſtinguiſhing *mark*, when purſued over the river *Jordan* by the *Ephraimites*.

The *eſſenes* among the *Jews*, (a ſort of *Pythagoreans)* alſo converſed one with another, by *ſigns* and *words*, which they received on their *admiſſion*, and which were preſerved with care and reverence, as the great characteriſtic of that ſect.

The * *Greeks* likewiſe had a particular method, which before an engagement, was adopted by the *general* and *officers*, and by them communicated, to the *whole* army, as a mark of diſtinction to know *friends* from *enemies*. It commonly contained ſome good *omen*, or the name of ſome *deity* worſhipped by their country; or ſome *hero* from whom they expected ſucceſs in their enterprizes. And it is judiciouſly remarked by LAERTIUS, that as generals uſe *watch-words* in order to diſcover their *own* ſoldiers from an *enemy*, (practiſed in all armies and garriſons at this day.) So it is neceſſary to communicate to the members of a *ſociety* certain diſtinctions whereby they may diſcover *ſtrangers* from individuals of their *own ſect*.

And is it not within the reach of every one's obſervation, that there is a meaning in many *acts* and *geſtures*; and that nature has endowed mankind with particular *motions* to expreſs the various intentions of the mind. We all underſtand ‡ *weeping*, *laughing*, *ſhrugs*, *frowns*, &c. as forming a ſpecies of *univerſal language*. Applications are many times made, and a kind of dia-

* But their *indiſcretion* in *too frequently* queſtioning one another, without *proper caution*, oft cauſed great confuſion among themſelves, and *diſcovered* the word *at laſt* to their enemies.

‡ Tears have the weight of a voice. OVID.

logue maintained only by the casts of the *eye*‡ and motions of the adjacent muscles; and we read even of *feet that speak*†; of a *philosopher*, who answered an argument only by *getting up* and *walking*‖.

Bending the knees, in adoration of the deity, is one of the most ancient customs among men. *Bowing*, or *prostrating the body*, is a mark of humiliation, Even joining *right* hands, is a pledge of fidelity; for *Valerius Maximus* tells us, that the ancients had a *moral deity*, whom they called FIDES, a goddess of *honesty* or *fidelity*, and adds, when they promised any thing of old, they *gave their hand* upon it, (as we do now) and therefore she is represented as giving her *hand*, and sometimes as only *two hands* conjoined. *Chartarius* more fully describes this, by observing, that the proper residence of *faith* or *fidelity*, was thought by the ancients to be in the *right hand*. And therefore this *deity*, he informs us, was sometimes represented by two *right hands* joined together; sometimes by two *little images* shaking each other's *right hand*; so that the *right hand* was by them held *sacred*, and was *symbolically* made use of in a solemn

‡ The *eyes*, the *eye-brows*, the *forehead*, in a word, the *whole countenance* is a certain tacit speech of the mind. CIC.

† He *speaketh* with his *feet*. (*Prov*. chap. vi. ver. 13)

‖ *Sextus Empiricus*.

manner

manner to denote *fidelity*. And we read in the *book* of *Ruth*, of particular customs practised among the *Israelites*, whenever *they* meant to *confirm* any compact they *entered* into.

With respect to PROBATIONARY DEGREES, the instances that might be produced of the *antiquity*, *necessity* and *general use* of *them*, would fill a large volume; suffice it here to mention the following.

The *philosophers* inform us, that the *Egyptian* king XOPPER, commanded, that the *secret* of which he was possessed, should not be divulged to any but those who were *found* skilful in *every step* they advanced: also the great heathen king XOPHOLET, ordered the *grand secret* of which he was possessed, to be revealed to none, but to those who after *thorough examination* were found to be *worthy*; and inflicted disgrace and severe punishments on those who should *transgress* this law.

And if we examine the customs of the *Jews*, we shall see that the *Levites* had the several degrees of *initiation*, *consecration* and *ministration*. And in their grand *sanhedrim*, they had also *three* chief officers, the *principal*, *vice principal*, and the *chacam*, (i. e. *wise man)* the last *two* were called *assistant councellors*. Their *pupils* were divided into *three* distinct *classes*, who according to their *abilities* were from time to time *elected* to fill up the vacant offices in this great assembly.

About the time of our SAVIOUR'S NATIVITY, the eastern schools used a set form of discipline.

The

The ſcholar was firſt termed *diſciple*, in reſpect of his learning; a *junior* in reſpect of his minority; *Bachur* (i. e. one *choſen* or *elected*) in reſpect of his election, and co-aptation into the number of diſciples. And after he had *proved* himſelf a proficient in their ſtudies, and was thought *worthy* of ſome degree, by impoſition of hands, he was made a *graduate*.

At the *eaſt* end of every *ſchool* or *ſynagogue*, the *Jews* had a cheſt called *Aaron* (or ark) in which was locked up the *pentateuch* in manuſcript, wrote on vellum, in *ſquare* characters, which by expreſs command, was to be delivered to *ſuch only* as were *found* to be *wiſe* among them, (2 *Eſdr*. c. xiv. v. 16.) This method of proceeding was alſo obſerved at the building of SOLOMON'S *temple*, when we know the *craftſmen* were not to be made *maſters*, until that glorious edifice ſhould be compleated, that ſo they might acquire *competent ſkill*, and be able to give AMPLE PROOF of their qualifications.

Pythagoras, who flouriſhed above 500 years before *Chriſt*, never permitted a pupil to ſpeak in his ſchool, till he had undergone a *probation* of *five years* ſilence.

The *eſſenes** already mentioned, had the following

* The *eſſenes* were men of excellent morals, eminent for their juſtice, beyond either *Greeks* or *Barbarians*, as a virtue that had been a long time their application and ſtudy. *Joſephus* lib. 18. c 12.

'Tis

lowing customs, when a person desired *admittance* into *their* society. He was to pass through proper degrees of *probation*, before he could be a *master* of their mysteries; when he was received into the class of *novices*, he was presented with a *white garment*, and when he had been long enough to give some *competent* proof of his *secrecy* and *virtue*, he was admitted to FURTHER knowledge, but still he went on with the trial of his *integrity* and good *morals*: and at *length*, being found worthy in every respect, was *fully* admitted into their *mysteries*; but before he was received as an established member, he was first to bind himself by solemn obligations and professions, to do justice, to do no wrong,

---

'Tis remarkable, that of the *three* famous sects among the *Jews* in the days of our LORD, *Pharisees*, *Sadduces* and *Essenes*, we find, tho' the first two *were* censured by *him*, the *Essenes* were *not*.

It is further related of this *sect*, they *were above all others strict observers of the sabbath day*; *on it they would dress no meat, light no fire, remove no vessels out of their places*, &c. (*Josephus*, *de Bello. lib.* I. c. 7.) Nay more, they observed every *seventh week* a *solemn pentacost* (Philo. de vita contemplat.) And if *Jews* without any divine *injunction* in this particular could *so* religiously observe the *sabbath*, how must *christians* stand condemned, who in flat disobedience to the *command* of an *omnipotent* GOD will not *devote* so much as one *day* in *seven* to honour *him* who gives them all things? All *free and accepted masons*, well know how great a violation of *our* principles every instance of such conduct is. And every *true* brother will be careful not to offend herein. *For by the fruit the tree is known.*

L to

to keep faith with all men, to embrace the truth, to keep his hand clear from fraudulent dealings, not to conceal from his fellow-professor, any of the *mysteries*, nor to communicate them to the *profane*, though it should be to *save his life*; to deliver nothing but what he received, as well as to endeavour to preserve the principles that he professed. Every member eat and drank at one common table, and any brethren of the same fraternity, who came from places ever so remote, were sure to be received at their meetings. (*Philo. de Vit. contemplat. Joseph. antiqu.* l. 8. c. 2.)

And it may be further remarked of the *Jews*, that in the feast of the seventh month, the High Priest was not even permitted to read the law to the people until he had studied it *seven days*, viz. upon the fourth, fifth, sixth, seventh, eighth, ninth, and tenth days, being attended by some of the priests to hear him perform and to judge of his *qualification* for that purpose. Vide † *Sir* Isaac Newton's *observations on the apocalypse of St. John.*

The above proceeding is so far from being *novel*, that it is practised in *our own nation* even at this day, in the *learned* societies of every denomination: For instance, in *accademical* degrees there are, *batchelor*, *master*, *doctor*; in the *church*, the several *orders* of *deacon*, *priest*, and *bishop*;

---

† These *seven days* are alluded to, by the Lamb's opening the *seven seals* successively.

in the *municipal law*, thoſe of *ſtudent*, *barriſter* and *ſerjeant*; in the *civil law and phyſick*, *ſtudent*, *batchelor* and *doctor*; in each of *theſe* the diſciple or ſcholar undergoes proper examinations, and muſt, or at leaſt *ought*, to be found well qualified *prior* to his admiſſion to a *ſuperior* rank.

And as FREE-MASONRY is in like manner a *progreſſive* ſcience, not to be perfectly attained but by *time*, *patience* and *application*, how neceſſary is it, that teſtimonies of proper qualifications ſhould be required for the reſpective *degrees*, before the candidate can attain them; both in regard to *ſcience* and *morality*; as the honour of the inſtitution ſhould always be a *principal* object in view to every *free and accepted maſon*, who ought to be well inſtructed in the *ſcientifick* knowledge, and *moral* and *ſocial* virtues peculiar to an *inferior**, e'er he will be admitted to the more

* Was a *contrary* practice to be adopted in our *gradations* in the craft, and *ſubſequent* degrees ſhould be conferred without taking due time to make proper trial of the *abilities*, *proficiency* and *morality* of the candidate; no one acquainted with our *conſtitution*, would heſitate a moment to pronounce *ſuch* practice an evident violation of its principles: and ſhould that ever prove to have been the caſe, it his hoped thoſe who erred therein, will inform themſelves of the great *impropriety* of ſuch proceedings; and think it a duty which they owe to the ſociety and to their *own Honour*, to diſcontinue ſuch practice, or they will give cauſe to ſuſpect that they wiſh not to regulate their proceedings by the *true* plan of *maſonry*.

ſublime truths of the *perfect* and *well qualified* MASON.

The nature of my deſign leads me in the next place to the conſideration of the *name* which has been adopted by our *inſtitution*, from its firſt eſtabliſhment; and to inform the unletter'd or inattentive brother, that this did *not* ariſe *merely* from our ſkill in *architecture*, or the *principles* of *building*, but from a more comprehenſive acquaintance and knowledge of the ſublimeſt principles of *philoſophy* and *moral virtues*; which however excellent they may be in the opinion of the learned and judicious part of mankind, cannot be indiſcriminately revealed to *every* one; leſt, inſtead of that reſpect which they require, for want of right underſtanding and a ſound mind, they might not produce their juſt and neceſſary conſequences; as even the *pureſt* morality and *wiſeſt* ſyſtems, have been too often ridiculed by the *folly* or *perverſeneſs* of *weak* or *wicked* men.

Therefore the name of *maſon* is not to be conſidered in the contracted implication of a builder of habitations, &c. But *figuratively** purſuant to the method of the *ancient ſociety* on which this *inſtitution* is founded; and taken in this ſenſe, a *maſon* is one who by

* The *apoſtles* alſo frequently made uſe of *this* Term in the like ſenſe, Acts xx. ver. 32. Epheſ. ii. ver. 22.

gradual advances in the ſublime *truths* and various *arts* and *ſciences* which the principles and precepts of *free-maſonry* tend to inculcate and eſtabliſh, is raiſed by regular *courſes* to ſuch a degree of perfection as to be replete with happineſs himſelf, and extenſively beneficial to others.

As to the appendage *free*, that evidently owed its riſe to the practice of the *ancients*, who never ſuffered the *liberal arts* and *ſciences* to be taught to any but the *free-born.*

I now preſume I have ſufficiently expoſed and everted *all* the foregoing allegations. And having alſo traced back to earlieſt ages, the *uſe* and meaning of *ſymbols* and *hieroglyphics*, and likewiſe fully demonſtrated the original *intention* and *uſe* of *allegorical* figures and ceremonies, and the reaſonableneſs and neceſſity of *progreſſive degrees* in the purſuit of *every* art and ſcience, no unprejudiced perſon will think it extraordinary that *thoſe* cuſtoms and ceremonies eſtabliſhed and connected with *our* inſtitution, have been moſt *ſacredly* and *inviolably* preſerved and adhered to by *us* to this day. But what ſuch cuſtoms and ceremonies *are*, for what ends and purpoſes *uſed*, never can be known except to *true* and *lawful brethren.*

Therefore, however anxious and reſtleſs the *buſy* and *invidious* may be, and whatever attempts *they* may make to *traduce* our inſtitution and proceedings, or *diſcover* our myſteries, all their endeavours

endeavours will prove ineffectual. They will ftill find that the *only* means to attain to the knowledge of our myfteries, are *abilities*, *integrity*, *firmnefs*, and a due and conftant perfeverance in the great duties of *moral* and *focial* life, in principles of *religion* and *virtue*, and whatever is commendable and praife-worthy. THESE are the fteps, and *this* the clue, that will lead and direct the practifers of fuch excellencies to the heights of *free-mafonry*, and while they adhere to them, will effectually fecure them favour and efteem from every able and faithful brother, and the warmeft approbation and fatisfaction from their own hearts.

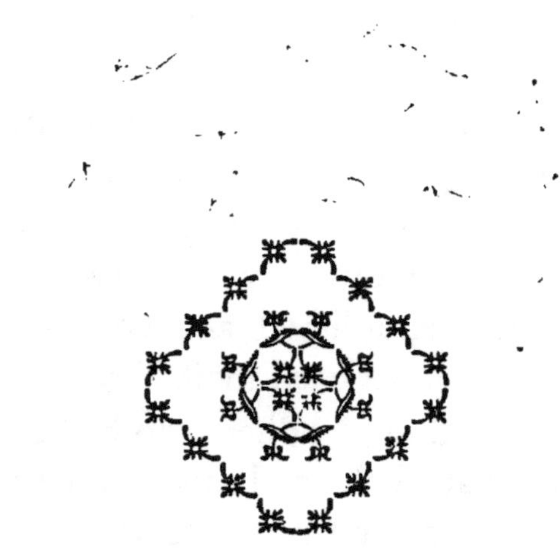

APPENDIX

APPENDIX.

HAVING ſhewn at what *period* and on what *plan*, FREE-MASONRY *firſt* became a regular *inſtitution*; I refer my readers to our book of excellent conſtitutions (which no *lodge* ought to be without) for a particular account of its progreſs in the various parts of the globe ever ſince. But as many may not have time and opportunity to conſult ſo ample a relation, I ſhall for the benefit of *ſuch*, take ſome notice *here* of the firſt eſtabliſhment of maſonry in this kingdom.

And notwithſtanding the obſurity which invelopes the hiſtory of the early ages of our country, various * circumſtances contribute to prove that

* The remains of ancient architecture of much earlier date than the *Romans*, the uſages and cuſtoms of the *Druid*'s, ſo exactly agreeable to the uſages of this *inſtitution*, which probably they gathered from the *Magians*, &c.

free-

free-masonry was introduced in *Britain* by the *first* inhabitants, and though many ancient records of this institution were either lost or destroyed in the wars of the *Saxons* and *Danes*, yet we are still possessed of ONE, which testifies that so far back as the reign of king ATHELSTONE, this fraternity were restored to, and confirmed in their ancient rights and privileges by a new charter or royal grant of that king, which is recorded in the old constitution, and relates that, " King ATHELSTONE, the grandson of ALFRED the great, a mighty architect, the first anointed king of England, and who translated the Holy Bible into the Saxon tongue, when he had brought the land into rest and peace, built many great works, and encouraged many masons from *France*, who were appointed overseers thereof, and brought with them the *charges* and *regulations* of the lodges, preserved since the *Roman* times, who also prevailed with the king to improve the constitution of the *English* lodges, according to the foreign model, and to encrease the wages of *working* masons. That the said king's brother, prince *Edwin*, being taught *masonry* and taking upon him the charges of a *master-mason*, for the love he had to the said craft, and the honourable principles whereon it is founded, purchased a *free charter* of his father for the *masons* to have a correction among themselves, (as it was anciently expressed,) or a freedom and power to regulate themselves, to

amend

amend what might happen amiſs within the craft, and to hold a yearly communication, and general aſſembly.

That accordingly prince *Edwin*, ſummoned all the maſons in the realm, to meet him in a congregation at *York*, in *June*, *A. D.* 926. who came and compoſed a general or grand lodge, of which he was Grand Maſter: And having brought with them all the old writings and records of the craft extant, ſome in *Greek*, ſome in *Latin*, ſome in *French*, and *other* languages, from the contents thereof, that aſſembly framed the *conſtitutions* and *charges* of an *Engliſh* lodge, made a law to preſerve and obſerve the ſame in all time coming, and ordained good pay for the working maſons."

And the craft was greatly encouraged by the *Saxon* and *Daniſh* monarchs, and other eminent and wealthy perſonages in ſucceeding ages; and wholeſome *laws* and *regulations* were occaſionally made and eſtabliſhed to promote and render permanent the proſperity, honour and harmony of the fraternity. For it is alſo recorded, that in the glorious reign of king *Edward* the *third*, who became the patron of *arts* and *ſciences*, the *charges* and *regulations* of maſons were, "reviſed and meliorated, and ſeveral new regulations were ordained;" from which time to the reign of king *Henry* the *ſixth*, maſonry continued in a flouriſhing ſtate, *lodges* and *communications* being more frequently held than ever, and tranquility, joy and felicity, univerſally abounded amongſt them.

This happy ſituation of the ſociety proved a ſufficient incitement with the *commons* of that day to attempt its overthrow, by a general ſuppreſſion of their *lodges* and *communications*; and taking advantage of the king's minority, in the *third* year of his reign, and the *fourth* of his age, an act was paſſed to prohibit, *their confederating in chapters or congregations.* But the prudent and upright deportment of the *brotherhood*, and the excellence of their principles, precepts, and regulations, had gained them ſuch univerſal eſteem, and good-will, that this *ſevere* edict, the effect of *envy* and *malevolence* in this arbitrary ſet of men, was never once executed, nor did it in the leaſt intimidate the maſons from holding their aſſemblies, or cauſe them to take any ſteps to get it repealed; conſcious of their own integrity, they dreaded not its force; on the contrary, we find, that in the minority of the ſame king, a very reſpectable lodge was held at *Canterbury*, and that a coat of arms, much the ſame with that of the London company of freemen-maſons, was uſed by them; whence it is natural to conceive, that the ſaid company is deſcended of the *ancient fraternity*; and that in former times, no man was made *free* of that *company*, until he was initiated in ſome lodge of *free and accepted maſons*, as a necaſſary qualification.

fication*. And it not only appears, that before the troubles which happened in the reign of this unfortunate prince, *free-masons* were universally esteemed, but even king *Henry* himself was made a mason in the year 1442, and many Lords and gentlemen of the court, after his example, solicited and obtained admission into the fraternity. And by *what follows*, we find how very intent this prince was to acquire some knowledge of the fundamental principles, history and traditions of the *Royal Art*, even *before* he was initiated; and from whence may also be gathered many of the original principles of the *ancient society*, on which the institution of *free-masonry* was ingrafted.

No doubt but every reader will feel some satisfaction in looking over this antique relation, though none more so than the *true* and *faithful brother*, in observing the glimmering conjectures of an *unenlightened* person, upon the fundamental principles, history and traditions of the *royal art*, though a philosopher of as great merit and penetration as this nation ever produced.

---

* This is the constant practice at this day amongst the *operative masons* in our sister kingdom, *Scotland*.

A letter from the learned Mr. John Locke, to the right Hon. Thomas Earl of Pembroke, with an old manuſcript on the ſubject of free-maſonry.

My Lord, *6th May*, 1696.

I Have at length, by the help of Mr Collins procured a copy of that M.S. in the Bodleian library, which you were ſo curious to ſee: and, in obedience to your Lordſhip's commands, I herewith ſend it to you. Moſt of the notes annexed to it, are what I made yeſterday for the reading of my lady Maſham, who is become ſo fond of maſonry, as to ſay, that ſhe now more than ever wiſhes herſelf a man, that ſhe might be capable of admiſſion into the fraternity.

The M. S. of which this is a copy, appears to be about 160 years old; yet (as your lordſhip will obſerve by the title) it is itſelf a copy of one yet more ancient by about 100 years: for the original is ſaid to have been the hand-writing of K. Henry VI. Where that prince had it is at preſent an uncertainty; but it ſeems to me to be an examination (taken perhaps before the king) of ſome one of the brotherhood of maſons; among whom he entred himſelf, as it is ſaid, when he came out of his minority, and thenceforth put a ſtop to a perſecution that had been raiſed againſt them: But I muſt not detain your lordſhip longer by my preface from the thing itſelf.

Certayne

Certayne questyons, with awnsweres to the same, concerning the mystery of maconrye; writtene by the hande of kynge Henrye the sixthe of the name, and faithfullye copyed by me (1) *Johan Leylande antiquarius, by the commaunde of his* (2) *highnesse.*

They be as followeth,

Quest. WHAT mote ytt be? (3)

Answ. Ytt beeth the skylle of nature, the understondynge of the myghte that ys hereynne, and its sondrye werckynges; sonderlyche, the skylle of rectenyngs, of waightes and metynges, and the treu manere of faconnynge al thynges for mannes use, headlye, dwellynges, and buyldynges of alle kindes, and al odher thynges that make gudde to manne.

---

(1) *John Leland* was appointed by Henry VIII. at the dissolution of monasteries, to search for, and save such books and records as were valuable among them. He was a man of great labour and industry.

(2) *His highnesse*, meaning the said king Henry VIII. Our kings had not then the title of majesty.

(3) *What mote ytt be?* That is, what may this mystery of masonry be? The answer imports, that it consists in natural, mathematical and mechanical knowledge. Some part of which (as appears by what follows) the masons pretend to have taught the rest of mankind, and some part they should conceal.

Quest.

Queſt. Where dyd ytt begyne?

Anſw. Ytt dyd begynne with the (4) fyrſte menne yn the eſte, whych were before the (5) ffyrſte manne of the weſt, and comynge weſtlye, ytt hathe brought herwyth alle comfortes to the wylde and comfortleſſe.

Queſt. Who dyd brynge ytt weſtlye?

Anſw. The (6) Venetians, whoo beynge grate merchandes, comed ffyrſt ffromme the eſte ynn Venetia, for the commodytye of marchaundyſynge beith eſte and weſte, bey the redde and myddlelonde ſees.

Queſt. Howe comede ytt yn Engelonde?

---

(4) (5) *Fyrſte menne yn the Eſte*, &c. It ſhould ſeem by this that maſons believe there were men in the eaſt before Adam, who is called the ffyrſte manne of the weſt; and that arts, and ſciences began in the eaſt. Some authors of great note for learning have been of the ſame opinion; and it is certain that Europe and Africa (which in reſpect to Aſia, may be called weſtern countries) were wild and ſavage, long after arts and politeneſs of manners were in great perfection in China, and the Indies.

(6) *The Venetians*, &c. In the time of monkiſh ignorance it is no wonder that the Phenicians ſhould be miſtaken for the Venetians. Or, perhaps, if the people were not taken one for the other, ſimilitude of ſound might deceive the clerk who firſt took down the examination. The Phenicians were the greateſt voyagers among the ancients, and were in Europe thought to be the inventors of letters, which perhaps they brought from the eaſt with other arts.

Anſw.

Answ. Peter Gower (7) a Grecian, journeyedde ffor kunnynge yn Egypte, and yn Syria, and yn everyche londe whereas the Venetians hadde plauntedde maconrye, and wynnynge entraunce yn al lodges of maconnes, he lerned muche, and retournedde, and woned yn Grecia magna (8)

---

(7) *Peter Gower*. This muſt be another miſtake of the writer. I was puzzled at firſt to gueſs who Peter Gower ſhould be, the name being perfectly Engliſh; or how a Greek ſhould come by ſuch a name: But as ſoon as I thought of Pythagoras, I could ſcarce forbear ſmiling, to find that philoſopher had undergone a metempſycoſis, he never dreamt of. We need only conſider the French pronounciation of his name, Pythagore, that is Petagore, to conceive how eaſily ſuch a miſtake might be made by an unlearned clerk. That Pythagoras travelled for knowledge into Egypt, &c. is known to all the learned; and that he was initated into ſeveral different orders of prieſts, who in thoſe days kept all their learning ſecret from the vulgar, is as well known. Pythagoras alſo, made every geometrical theorem a ſecret, and admitted only ſuch to the knowledge of them, as had firſt undergone a five years ſilence. He is ſuppoſed to be the inventor of the XLVII. propoſition of the firſt book of Euclid, for which, in the joy of his heart, it is ſaid he ſacrificed a hecatomb. He alſo knew the true ſyſtem of the world, lately revived by Copernicus; and was certainly a moſt wonderful man. See his life by Dion Hall.

(8) *Grecia Magna*, a part of Italy formerly ſo called, in which the Greeks had ſettled a large colony.

wachſynge,

wachſynge, and becommynge a myghtye (9) wyſeacre, and greatelyche renowned, and her he framed a grate lodge at Groton (10) and maked many maconnes, ſome whereoffe dyd jeurneye yn Fraunce, and maked many maconnes, wherefromme, yn proceſſe of tyme, the arte paſſed yn Engelonde.

Queſt. Dothe maconnes deſcouer here artes unto odhers?

Anſw. Peter Gower whenne he journeyedde to lernne, was ffyrſte (11) made, and anonne techedde; evenne ſoe ſhulde all odhers beyn recht. Natheleſs (12) maconnes hauethe always yn everyche tyme from tyme to tyme communycatedde to

---

(9) *Wyſeacre.* This word at preſent ſignifies ſimpleton, but formerly had a quite contrary meaning. Weiſager in the old Saxon, is philoſopher, wiſeman or wizard, and having been frequently uſed ironically, at length came to have a direct meaning in the ironical ſenſe. Thus, Duns Scotus, a man famed for the ſubtility and acuteneſs of his underſtanding, has by the ſame method of irony, given a general name to modern dunces.

(10) *Groton.* Groton is the name of a place in England. The place here meant is Crotona, a city of Grecia Magna, which in the time of Pythagoras was very populous.

(11) *Fyrſte made.* The word *made* I ſuppoſe has a particular meaning among the maſons: perhaps it ſignifies, initiated.

(12) *Maconnes haueth communycatedde*, &c. This paragraph hath ſomething remarkable in it. It contains a juſtification of

to mannkynde ſoche of her ſecrettes as generallyche myghte be uſefulle; they haueth keped backe ſoche allein as ſhulde be harmefulle yff they comed yn euylle haundes, oder ſoche as ne myghte be holpynge wythouten the techynges to be joinedde herwythe in the lodge, oder ſoche as do bynde the freres more ſtrongelyche togeder, bey the proffytte and commodytye comyng to the confrerie herfromme.

Queſt. Whatte artes haueth the maconnes techedde mankynde?

Anſw. The artes (13) agricultura, architectura aſtronomia, geometria, numeres, muſica, poeſe, kymiſtry, governmente, and relygyonne.

Queſt. Howe commethe maconnes more teachers than odher menne;

Anſw. The hemſelfe haueth allein in (14) arte of

---

of the ſecrecy ſo much boaſted of by maſons, and ſo much blamed by others; aſſerting that they have in all ages diſcovered ſuch things as might be uſeful, and that they conceal ſuch only as would be hurtful either to the world or themſelves. What theſe ſecrets are, we ſee afterwards.

(13) *The arts, agriculture,* &c. It ſeems a bold pretence this of the maſons, that they have taught mankind all theſe arts. They have their own authority for it; and I know not how we ſhall diſprove them. But what appears moſt odd, is, that they reckon religion among the arts.

(14) *Arte of ffynding neue artes.* The art of inventing arts, muſt certainly be a moſt uſeful art. My lord Bacon's Novum Organum is an attempt towards ſomething of the ſame kind.

of fynding neue artes, whyche arte the ffyrste maconnes receaued from Godde; by the whyche they fyndethe whatte artes hem plesethe, and the treu way of techynge the same. Whatt odher mennedoethe ffynde out, ys onelythe bey chaunce and therfore but lytel I tro.

Quest. Whatt dothe the maconnes concele and hyde?

Answ. They concelethe the art of ffyndynge neue artrs, and thattys for her own proffytte, and (15) preise: They concelethe the art of kepynge (16) secrettes, thatt soe the worlde mayeth nothinge concele from them. They concelethe the art of wunderwerckynge, and of foresayinge thynges to come, thatt so thay same artes may not be usedde of the wyckedde to an euyell

---

kind. But I much doubt, that if ever the masons had it, they have now lost it; since so few new arts have been lately invented, and so many are wanted. The idea I have of such an art is, that it must be something proper to be applied in all the sciences, generally, as algebra is in numbers, by the help of which, new rules of arithmetic are, and may be found.

(15) *Preise.* It seems the masons have great regard to the reputation as well as the profit of their order; since they make it one reason for not divulging an art in common, that it may do honour to the professors of it. I think in this particular they shew too much regard for their own society, and too little for the rest of mankind.

(16) *Arte of keepynge secrettes.* What kind of an art this is, I can by no means imagine. But certainly such an art the masons

euyell ende; they alſo concelethe the (17) arte of chaunges, the wey of wynnynge the facultye (18) of Abrac, the ſkylle of becommynge gude and perfyghte wythouten the holpynges of fere, and hope; and the universelle (19) longage of maconnes.

---

maſons muſt have: For though, as ſome people ſuppoſe, they ſhould have no ſecret at all, even that muſt be a ſecret which being diſcovered would expoſe them to the higheſt ridicule: and therefore it requires the utmoſt caution to conceal it.

(17) *Arte of chaunges.* I know not what this means, unleſs it be the tranſmutation of metals.

(18) *Facultye of Abrac.* Here I am utterly in the dark.

(19) *Universelle lingage of maconnes.* An univerſal language has been much deſired by the learned of many ages. It is a thing rather to be wiſhed than hoped for. But it ſeems the maſons pretend to have ſuch a thing among them. If it be true, I gueſs it muſt be ſomething like the language of the Pantomimes among the ancient Romans, who are ſaid to be able, by ſigns only, to expreſs and deliver any oration intelligibly to men of all nations and languages. A man who has all theſe arts and advantages, is certainly in a condition to be envied: But we are told, that this is not the caſe with all maſons; for though theſe arts are among them, and all have a right and opportunity to know them, yet ſome want capacity, and others induſtry to acquire them. However, of all their arts and ſecrets, that which I deſire moſt to know is, *The ſkyle of becommynge gude and perfyghte*; and I wiſh it were communicated to all mankind, ſince there is nothing more true than the beautiful ſentence contained in the laſt anſwer, " The better men are, the more they love one another." Virtue having in itſelf ſomething ſo amiable as to charm the hearts of all that behold it.

Quest. Wylle he teche me thay ſame artes ?

Anſw. Ye ſhalle be techedde yff ye be warthye, and able to lerne.

Queſt. Dothe all maconnes kunne more then odher menne ?

Anſw. Not ſo. Thay onlyche haueth recht and occaſyonne more then odher menne to kunne, but manye doeth fale yn capacity, and manye more doth want induſtrye, thatt ys perneceſſarye for the gaynynge all kunnynge.

Queſt. Are maconnes gudder men then odhers ?

Anſw. Some maconnes are not ſo vertuous as ſome other menne ; but yn the moſte parte, thay be more gude than they woulde be yf thay war not maconnes.

Queſt. Doth maconnes love eidther odher myghtylye as beeth ſayde ?

Anſw. Yea verylyche, and yt may not odherwiſe be : For gude menne and treu, kennynge eidher odher to be ſoche, doeth always love the more as thay be more gude.

Here endethe the queſtyonnes, and awnſwers.

I know not what effect the ſight of this old paper may have upon your lordſhip ; but for my own part I cannot deny, that it has ſo much raiſed my curioſity, as to induce me to enter myſelf into the fraternity, which I am determined to do (if I may be admitted) the next time I go to London, and that will be ſhortly. I am,

My Lord,

Your Lordſhip's moſt obedient,

And moſt humble ſervant,

A Gloſſary *to explain the old words in the foregoing manuſcript.*

ALLEIN, only
Alweys, always
Beithe, both
Commodytye, conveniency
Confrerie, fraternity
Faconnynge, forming
Fore-ſayinge, prophecying
Freres, brethren
Headlye, chiefly
Hem pleſethe, they pleaſe
Hemſelfe, themſelves
Her, there, their
Hereynne, therein
Herwyth, with it
Holpynge, beneficial
Kunne, know
Kunnynge, knowledge
Make gudde, are beneficial
Metynges, meaſures
Mote, may
Myddlelonde, Mediterranean
Myghte, power
Occaſyonne, opportunity
Oder, or
Onelyche, only
Perneceſſarye, abſolutely neceſſary
Preiſe, honour
Recht, right,
Reckenyngs, numbers
Sonderlyche, particularly
Skylle, knowledge
Wackſynge, growing
Werck, operation
Wey, way
Whereas, where
Woned, dwelt
Wunderwerckynge, working miracles
Wylde, ſavage
Wynnynge, gaining
Ynn, into

It would be next to an impoſſibility to enumerate all the Royal, Noble, and Eminent perſonages, who have thought it no diminution of their dignities to protect and patronize the *craft*, and to preſide as GRAND MASTERS over the fraternity in different parts of the globe. However, the following catalogue of thoſe who have ſat in SOLOMON's chair in *this* kingdom*, together with their DEPUTIES and *provincial* GRAND MASTERS for near 50 years paſt, may not be unacceptable to the reader, and at the ſame time muſt put to ſilence and ſhame any who look upon *free-maſonry*, as a trifling inſtitution.

1721. *John Montague*, duke of Montague, grand maſter.

John Beal, doctor of phyſic, deputy grand maſter.

1722. *Philip Wharton*, duke of Wharton, grand maſter

J. Theo. Deſaguliers, L. L. D. and F. R. S. deputy grand maſter.

1723. *F. Scott*, E. of Dalkieth, late duke of Buccleugh, grand maſter.

J. Theo. Deſaguliers, L. L. D. and F. R. S. deputy grand maſter.

1724. *C. Lenox*, duke of Richmond, Lenox, and Aubigny, grand maſter.

* For the Grand Maſters in *Scotland*, Vide. further on.

Martin

Martin Folkes, Efq; deputy grand mafter.

1725. *J. Hamilton*, Lord Paifley, now E. of Abercorn, grand mafter.

J. Theo. Defaguliers, L. L. D. and F. R. S. deputy grand mafter.

1726. *William Obrian*, earl of Inchiquin, grand mafter.

William Cowper, Efq; deputy grand mafter.

1727. *Henry Hare*, lord Coleraine, grand mafter.

Alexander Chocke, Efq; deputy grand mafter.

1728. *James King*, Lord Kingfton, grand mafter.

Nathaniel Blackerby, Efq; deputy grand mafter.

1729-30. *Thomas Howard*, duke of Norfolk, grand mafter.

Nathaniel Blackerby, Efq; deputy grand mafter.

1731. *T. Cooke*, Ld. Lovel, afterwards E. of Leicefter, grand mafter.

Thomas Batfon, Efq; deputy grand mafter.

1732. *Anthony Brown*, lord Vifc. Montacute, grand mafter.

Thomas Batfon, Efq; deputy grand mafter.

1733. *James Lyon*, earl of Strathmore, grand mafter.

Thomas Batfon, Efq; deputy grand mafter.

1734. *John Lindfay*, E. of Crawford, primier earl of Scotland, grand mafter.

Sir Cecil Wray, Bart. deputy grand mafter.

1735.

1735. *Thomas Thynne*, Ld. Visc. Weymouth, grand master.

John Ward, Esq; deputy grand master.

1736 *John Campbell*, earl of Loudoun, grand master.

John Ward, Esq; deputy grand master.

1737. *Edward Bligh*, earl of Darnley, grand master.

John Ward, Esq; deputy grand master.

1738. *H. Bridges*, marq. of Carnarvon, now D. of Chandos, grand master.

John Ward, Esq; deputy grand master.

1739. *Robert Raymond*, lord Raymond, grand master.

William Græme, Dr. of physick, deputy grand master.

1740. *John Keith*, earl of Kintore, grand master.

William Græme, Dr. of physic, deputy grand master.

1741-2. *J. Douglass*, E. of Morton, Kt. of the thistle, grand master.

Martin Clare, M. A. and F. R. S. deputy grand master.

1743-4. *John Ward*, now lord Viscount Dudley and Ward, grand master.

Sir Robert Lawley, Bart, deputy grand master.

1745-6. *Thomas Lyon*, earl of Strathmore, grand master.

William Vaughan, Esq; deputy grand master.

1747-8. *James Cranstoun*, lord Cranstoun, grand master.

Edward Hody, Dr. of phyfic, and F. R. S. deputy grand mafter.

1749-50-1. *William Byron*, lord Byron, grand mafter.

Fotherley Baker, Efq; deputy grand mafter.

1752. *John Proby*, lord Carysfort, grand mafter.

Thomas Manningham, Dr. of phyfic, deputy grand mafter.

1754. *James Bridges*, marq. of Carnarvon, fon and heir to Henry Duke of Chandos, formerly grand mafter, grand mafter.

Thomas Manningham, Dr. of phyfic, deputy grand mafter.

1757. *Sholto Charles Douglafs*, lord Aberdour, now earl of Morton, grand mafter.

Mr. John Revis, deputy grand mafter.

1762. *Wafhington Shirley*, earl Ferrers, grand mafter.

Mr. John Revis, deputy grand mafter.

1764. *Cadwallader*, lord Blaney, grand mafter.

Col. John Salter, deputy grand mafter.

1767. *Henry Somerfet*, Duke of Beaufort, grand mafter.

The Honourable Charles Dillon, Efq; deputy grand mafter.

DEPUTATIONS for PROVINCIAL GRAND-MASTERS were granted,

In 1726, by Lord *Paisley*, grand master,

To Sir *Edward Mansell*, Baronet, for South Wales.

Hugh Warburton, Esquire, for North Wales.

In 1728, by Lord *Kingston*, grand master.

To *George Pomfret*, Esquire, for Bengal, in the East-Indies.

1729, by the Duke of *Norfolk*, grand master.

To Captain *Ralph Farwinter*, for the East-Indies.

Monsieur *Thuanus*, for the circle of Lower Saxony.

Mr. *Daniel Cox*, for New Jersey, in America.

In 1731, by Lord *Lovell*, late Earl of *Leicester*, grand master.

To Captain *John Phillips*, for all the Russias.

Captain *James Commerford*, for the Province of Andalusia, in Spain.

Sir *Edward Matthews* for Shropshire.

In 1734, by the Earl of *Crawfurd*, grand master.

To *Edward Entwizle*, Esquire for Lancashire.

Joseph Laycock, Esquire, for Durham.

Matthew Ridley, Esquire, for Northumberland.

In 1736, by the Earl of *Loudoun*, grand master.

To *Robert Tomlinson*, Esquire, for New-England.

John Hammerton, Esquire, for South Carolina.

David Creighton, M. D. for Cape Coast in Africa.

In

In 1737, by the Earl of *Darnley*, grand maſter.

To *James Watſon*, Eſquire, for the Iſland of Montſerrat.

George Hamilton, Eſquire, for the State of Geneva.

Henry William Marſhalch, Eſquire, Hereditary Mareſchal of Thuringia, for Upper Saxony.

William Douglas, Eſquire, for the Coaſt of Africa and Iſlands of America, where no particular deputation had been granted.

Richard Riggs, Eſquire, for New York.

In 1738, by the Marquis of *Carnarvon*, now Duke of *Chandois*, grand maſter.

To *William Horton*, Eſquire, for the Weſt Riding of the County of York.

His Excellency Governor *Matthew*, for the Leeward Iſlands.

In 1739, by Lord *Raymond*, grand maſter.

To the Marquis *Des Marches*, for Savoy and Piedmont.

In 1740, by the Earl of *Kintore*, grand maſter.

To his Excellency *James Keith*, for all the Ruſſias.

Matthew Albert Luttman, Eſquire, for Hamburgh, and the Circle of Lower Saxony.

Edward Rooke, Eſquire, for the Weſt Riding of the County of York, in the room of William Horton, Eſq; deceaſed.

Thomas Baxter, Eſquire, his Majeſty's Attorney-General, for the Iſland of Barbadoes, and of all the Iſlands to the Windward

In 1742, by Lord *Ward*, now Viſcount Dudley, grand maſter.

To Mr. *William Ratchdale*, for the County of Lancaſter.

Ballard Beckford, *George Hynde*, and *Alexander Crawford*, Eſquires, for the Iſland of Jamaica.

Thomas Oxnard, Eſquire, for North America.

In 1744, by the Earl of *Strathmore*, grand maſter.

To *Alured Popple*, Eſquire, for Bermudas,

In 1746, by Lord *Cranſtoun*, grand maſter.

To Captain *Commins*, for Cape-Breton and Louiſburgh.

In 1747, 1748, 1749, 1750, 1751, by Lord *Byron*, grand maſter.

To *William Allen*, Eſquire, Recorder of Philadelphia, for Penſilvania, in America.

Count *Denneſkiold Laurwig*, for Denmark and Norway.

Lieutenant Colonel *James Adolphus Oughton*, for the Iſland of Minorca.

Francis Goelet, Eſquire, for the Province of New York.

In 1752, 1753, by Lord *Caryſfort*, grand maſter.

To *William Pye*, Eſquire, for the County of Cornwall.

James Montriſor, Eſquire, for Gibraltar.

His Excellency Governor *Tinker*, for the Bahama Iſlands.

Sir *Robert de Cornwall*, Baronet, for the Counties of Worceſter, Glouceſter, Salop, Monmouth, and Hereford.

George

George Harrison, Esquire, for the Province of New York.

Thomas Dorree, Esquire, for Guernsey, Jersey, Alderney, Sark, and Arme, in the British Channel.

In 1754, 1755, by the Marquis of *Carnarvon*, grand master.

To *Peter Leigh*, Esquire, Chief Justice of South Carolina, for South Carolina.

David Jones Gwynne, of Talliaries, Esquire, for South Wales, in the room of Sir Edward Mansell.

The Reverend and Honourable *Frances Byam*, D. D. for Antigua.

The Honourable *Roger Drake*, Esquire, at Bengal, for East India.

Jeremiah Gridley, Esquire, for all North America, where no Provincial is appointed.

William Maynard, Esquire, for Barbadoes, and all other his Majesty's Islands to the Windward of Guardaloup.

Edward Galliard, Esquire, for St. Eustatius, Saba, and St. Martin, Dutch Carribbee Islands in America.

John Head, Gent. Collector of the Customs at Scilly, for Scilly, and the adjacent Islands.

Jobst Anthony Hinuber, for all his Majesty's Dominions in Germany, with a Power to choose Successors.

John Page, of Hawthorn, Esquire, for the

County

County Palatine of Chester, and the City and County of Chester.

In 1758, 1759, 1760, by Lord *Aberdour*, grand master.

To *William Jarvis*, Esquire, for Antigua.

Edward Bacon, Esquire, for Norwich, and the County of Norfolk.

James Bradford, Esquire, for the Bahama Islands.

Gottfried Jacob Jenisch, M. D. for Hamburgh and Lower Saxony.

John Smith, Esq; for the County of Lancaster.

Grey Elliot, Esq; for Georgia.

In 1761, 1762, by Lord *Carysfort*, grand master.

To *William Vaughan*, Esq; for North Wales.

John Lewis, for Andalusia, and places adjacent.

Benjamin Smith, Esquire, for Carolina.

Thomas Marriott Perkins, Esq; for the Musqueta Shore.

In 1763, by Earl *Ferrers*, grand master.

To *Cutting Smith*, Esq; for East India.

Thomas Marriott Perkins, Esq; for Jamaica.

In 1764, 1765, by Lord *Blaney*, grand master.

To Captain *John Blewitt*, for East India, where no other is appointed.

Doctor *Dyonysius Manasse*, for Armenia.

George Augustus, Baron of Hammerstein, for Westphalia.

James Tod, Esq; for Bombay.

Ernest Siegmond de Lestwitz, for the Dukedom of Brunswick.

His Excellency *Robert Melville*, Esquire, for the Greater and Lesser Granadoes, St. Vincent, Dominica, Tobago, &c.

Millborne West, Esq; for Canada.

John Stone, Esquire, for Barbadoes.

John George Henry Count de Werthen, for Upper Saxony.

In 1767, by his Grace *Henry Duke of Beaufort*, grand master.

John Smith, Esq; (member of parliament) for Somersetshire.

The honourable *Boyle Walsingham*, (member of parliament) for Kent.

J. J. De Vignoles, for foreign lodges, where no provincial is appointed.

An Account of the ESTABLISHMENT *of the* PRESENT *Grand Lodge of* SCOTLAND.

THE fraternity of FREE-MASONS in Scotland always owned their king and ſovereign as their grand-maſter: To his authority they ſubmitted all diſputes that happened amongſt the brethren. When not a *maſon* himſelf, he appointed one of the brethren to preſide as his deputy at all their meetings, and to regulate all matters concerning the *craft*. Accordingly we find James I. 1430, that patron of learning, countenancing the lodges with his preſence, "as the royal grand-maſter; "till he ſettled an yearly revenue of four pounds "Scots, to be paid by every maſter maſon in "Scotland, to a grand maſter choſen by the "brethren, and approved of by the crown, one "nobly born, or an eminent clergyman, who "had his deputies in cities and counties; and "every new brother at entrance paid him alſo a "fee. His office empowered him to regulate

in

" in the fraternity what ſhould not come under " the cognizance of law-courts; to him appeal- " ed both *maſon* and *lord*, or the *builder* and " *founder* when at variance, in order to prevent " law-pleas; and in his abſence they appealed to " his deputy or grand-wardens that reſided " next to the premiſes."

1441. William St. Clair, earl of Orkney and Caithneſs, baron of Roſlin, *&c. &c.* got a grant of this office from king James II. He countenanced the lodges with his preſence, propagated the royal art, and built the chapel of Roſlin, that maſter-piece of Gothic architecture. Maſonry now began to ſpread its benign influence through the country, and many noble and ſtately buildings were reared by the prince and nobles during the time of grand-maſter Roſlin. By another deed of the ſaid king James II. this office was made hereditary to the ſaid William St. Clair, and his heirs and ſucceſſors in the barony of Roſlin: in which noble family it has continued without any interruption till of late years. The barons of Roſlin have ever ſince continued to prove the patrons of maſonry, in countenancing the lodges, determining in all matters of difference amongſt the brethren, and ſupporting with becoming dignity the character of grand-maſter maſon over all *Scotland*. They held their head court (or in maſon ſtyle) aſſembled their grand lodge at Kilwinning in the weſt country, where it is preſumed maſons firſt began in Scotland to

 hold

hold regular and ſtated lodges. Nay, it is even alledged, that in this * place the royal art *firſt* made its appearance, and the brethren, meeting here with hoſpitality and protection, formed themſelves into a lodge; and their peaceable behaviour, their hoſpitable and generous diſpoſitions, recommending them to the notice of the country, they were ſoon aſſociated by the great and wealthy from all parts. In proceſs of time the craft became more numerous, and lodges more frequent throughout the country; the lodge of Kilwinning, under authority of the noble grand-maſters, granting charters of erection and conſtitution to the brethren to form themſelves into regular lodges, always under the proper proviſions and reſtrictions, for their adhering to the ſtrict principles of true old maſonry, and preſerving amongſt themſelves that harmony and union which ought, and always has ſubſiſted amongſt the fraternity.

Such continued to be the ſtate of maſonry, whilſt the family of Roſlin were in flouriſhing and proſperous circumſtances: but that once opulent and noble family, through their too great generoſity, falling back in the world, the preſent re-

* Thoſe who mean any thing *more* by *Kilwinning* maſons, than that they are of the body of maſons, which *firſt* formed themſelves into a regular inſtitution at *Kilwinning*, muſt be miſtaken. The *grand lodge* at *Edingburgh* always toaſt the lodge of *Kilwinning* as their *mother lodge*.

preſentative

presentative William Sinclair of Roslin, Esq; (a real mason, and a gentleman of the greatest candour and benevolence, inheriting his predecessors virtues without their fortune) was obliged to dispone the estate; and, having no children of his own, was loth that the office of *grand master*, now vested in his person, should become vacant at his death: more especially, as there was but small prospect of the brethren of this country receiving any countenance or protection from the crown (to whom the office naturally reverted, at the failure of the Roslin family,) as in ancient days, our kings and princes continually residing in England.

Upon these considerations, (October 15, 1736.) having assembled the brethren of the lodges in and about Edinburgh, grand-master St. Clair represented to them how beneficial it would be to the cause of masonry in general to have a grand-master, a gentleman or nobleman of their own country, one of their own electing, to patronize and protect the craft; and that, as hereditary *grand-master* over all Scotland, he had called this meeting, in order to condescend on a proper plan for electing of a *grand-master*; and that in order to promote so laudable a design, he proposed to resign into the hands of the brethren, or whomsoever they should be pleased to elect, all right, claim, or title whatever, which he or his successors have to reign as grand-master over the masons in Scotland; and recommended to the

P 2 brethren,

brethren, to look out for a *nobleman* or *gentleman*, one of the craft, fit to ſucceed his *noble* predeceſſors, a man qualified to patronize and protect the ſociety, and ſupport the character of *grand-maſter* with the honour and dignity becoming that high ſtation; and concluded with recommending to them unanimity, harmony, and brotherly love, in all their proceedings thereanent.

The brethren taking into conſideration what the grand-maſter had above repreſented, reſolved upon proper rules and regulations, to be obſerved in the election of a grand-maſter againſt St. *Andrew's* day next; and that they might not be ſaid to take any ſtep without the countenance and approbation of the more diſtant lodges, they ordered the following letter to be wrote to all the lodges throughout Scotland, inviting them to appear by themſelves or proxies, in order to concur in promoting ſo laudable a ſcheme.

BRETHREN,

"THE four lodges in and about Edinburgh "having taken to their ſerious conſidera-"tion, the great loſs that maſonry has ſuſtained "thro' the want of a grand-maſter, authorized "us to ſignify to you, our good and worthy bre-"thren, our hearty deſire and firm intention, "to chuſe a grand-maſter for *Scotland*; and in "order the ſame may be done with the greateſt "harmony, we hereby invite you (as we have

"done

" done all the other regular lodges known by
" us,) to concur in ſuch a great and good work,
" whereby it is hoped *maſonry* may be reſtored
" to its ancient luſtre in this kingdom: And
" for effectuating this laudable deſign, we hum-
" bly deſire, that, betwixt and Martinmas day
" next, you will be pleaſed to give us a brotherly
" anſwer in relation to the election of a *grand-*
" *maſter*, which we propoſe to be on St. *An-*
" *drew's* day, for the firſt time, and ever there-
" after to be upon St. *John the Baptiſt's* day, or
" as the grand lodge ſhall appoint by the ma-
" jority of voices, which are to be collected
" from the maſters and wardens of all the regu-
" lar lodges then preſent, or by proxy to any
" maſter-maſon or fellow-craft in any lodge in
" *Scotland*: And the election is to be in *Mary's*
" *Chapel*. All that is hereby propoſed is for
" the advancement and proſperity of maſonry
" in its greateſt and moſt charitable perfection.
" We hope and expect a ſuitable return; wherein
" if any lodge are defective, they have them-
" ſelves only to blame. We heartily wiſh you
" all manner of ſucceſs and proſperity, and ever
" are, with great reſpect, your affectionate and
" loving brethren, *&c.*

(Mary's Chapel. Nov. 30. 1736.)

This day being appointed for the election of a *grand-maſter* and other officers to compoſe the grand lodge of *Scotland*, the following lodges appeared by themſelves or proxies: viz.

Mary's

Mary's Chapel,
Kilwinning,
Canongate Kilwining,
Kilwinning Scots arms,
Kilwinning Leith,
Kilwinning Glaſgow,
Cupar of Fife,
Linlithgow,
Dumfermline,
Dundee,
Dalkieth,
Aitcheſon's haven,
Selkirk,
Inverneſs,
Laſmahego,
St. Bride's at Douglas,
Strathaven,
Hamilton,
Lanerk,
Dunſe,
Kirkaldie,
Journeymen maſons, Edin.
Kirkentulloch,
Biggar,
Sanquhar,
Peebles,
Glaſgow St. Mungo's,
Greenock,
Falkirk,
Aberdeen,
Canongate and Leith,
Leith and Canong.
Montroſe.

When the lodge was duly met, and the rolls called over, there was produced the following reſignation of the office of grand-maſter, by William St. Clair of Roſlin, Eſq; in favour of the brethren, or whomſoever they ſhould be pleaſed to elect to that high office.

" I William St. Clair of Roſlin, Eſq; taking " to my conſideration, that the maſons in " Scotland did, by ſeveral deeds, conſtitute and " appoint William and Sir William St. Clairs of " Roſlin, my anceſtors, and their heirs, to be " their patrons, protectors, judges or maſters;

" and

" and that my holding or claiming any ſuch ju-
" riſdiction, right or privilege, might be preju-
" dicial to the *craft* and *vocation* of *maſonry*,
" whereof I am a member; and I being deſirous
" to advance and promote the good and utility
" of the ſaid craft of maſonry to the utmoſt of
" my power, do therefore hereby, for me and
" my heirs, renounce, quit claim, overgive and
" diſcharge all right, claim or pretence that I,
" or my heirs, had, have, or any ways may have,
" pretend to, or claim, to be patron, protector,
" judge or maſter of the maſons in Scotland, in
" virtue of any deed or deeds made and granted
" by the ſaid maſons, or of any grant or charter
" made by any of the kings of Scotland, to and
" in favours of the ſaid William and Sir William
" St. Clairs of Roſlin, my predeceſſors; or any
" other manner of way whatſoever, for now
" and ever: And I bind and oblige me, and my
" heirs, to warrant this preſent renunciation and
" diſcharge at all hands: And I conſent to the
" regiſtration hereof in the books of council and
" ſeſſion, or any other judges books competent;
" therein to remain for preſervation; and there-
" to I conſtitute

my procurators, &c.

" in witneſs whereof I have ſubſcribed theſe pre-
" ſents (written by David Maul writer to the
" ſignet) at Edinburgh, the twenty fourth day
" of November, one thouſand ſeven hundred
" and *thirty ſix years*, before theſe witneſſes,
" George Fraſer deputy-auditor of the exciſe

" in Scotland, maſter of the Canongate lodge
" and William Montgomery merchant in Leith,
" maſter of the Leith lodge.

WM. ST. CLAIR.

Geo. Fraſer, Canongate Kilwinning, witneſs,
Wm. Montgomery, Leith Kilwinning, witneſs.
Which being read, was ordered to be recorded in the books to be hereafter kept in the grand lodge of *Scotland*.

After this the brethren proceeded to the election of a *grand-maſter*; and, in conſideration of his noble and ancient family, for the zeal he himſelf had now ſhown for the good and proſperity of the craft, they thought they could not confer that high honour upon any brother better qualified, or more properly entitled, than William St. Clair of Roſlin, Eſq; whoſe anceſtors had ſo long preſided over the brethren, and had ever acquitted themſelves with honour and with dignity. Accordingly,

By an unanimous voice, William St. Clair of Roſlin, Eſq; was proclaimed *grand-maſter-maſon* of all *Scotland*, and being placed in the chair, was inſtalled, ſaluted, homaged and acknowledged as ſuch.

Now we come to thoſe halcyon days, when maſonry began to flouriſh in *Scotland* in harmony, reputation and numbers; and many noblemen and gentlemen of the firſt rank, beſides other learned men, merchants, clergymen and tradeſmen, deſired to be admitted into the fraternity;

ternity; and finding a lodge to be a safe and pleasant relaxation from intense study or hurry of business, without politicks or party, took great pleasure and delight therein.

We shall now proceed to the recital of those *great* personages who have thought it their honour, to preside as grand-masters, or other officers of the grand lodge; and we congratulate the brethren on the happy prospect they still have of honourable and worthy brothers succeeding to SOLOMON'S chair, and presiding as grand-masters over them; under whose benign influence, may the craft continue to flourish and increase; may they be eminent and distinguished amongst mankind, for harmony and virtue, as belonging to *a society* dedicated for promoting these great and valuable purposes.

Nov. 30, 1736. *William St. Clair*, of Roslin, Esq; grand master.
Captain John Young, deputy grand master.

1737. *George earl of Cromarty*, grand master.
Captain John Young, deputy grand master.

1738. *John earl of Kintore*, grand master.
Captain John Young, deputy grand master.

1739. *James earl of Morton*, grand master.
Captain John Young, deputy grand master.

1740. *Thomas earl of Strathmore and Kinghorn*, grand master.
Captain John Young, deputy grand master.

1741. *Alexander earl of Leven*, grand master,

Captain John Young, deputy grand maſter.

1742. *William earl of Kilmarnock*, grand maſter.

Captain John Young, deputy grand maſter.

1743. *James earl of Weemyſs*, grand maſter.

Captain John Young, deputy grand maſter.

1744. *James earl of Murray*, grand maſter.

Captain John Young deputy grand maſter.

1745. *Henry David earl of Buchan*, grand maſter.

Captain John Young, deputy grand maſter.

1746. *William Niſbet of Dirleton*, Eſq; grand maſter.

Major John Young, deputy grand maſter.

1747. *Francis Charteris of Amesfield*, Eſq; grand maſter.

Major John Young, deputy grand maſter.

1748. *Hugh Seton of Touch*, Eſq; grand maſter.

Major John Young, deputy grand maſter.

1749. *Thomas lord Erſkine*, grand maſter.

Major John Young, deputy grand maſter.

1750. *Alexander earl of Eglinton*, grand maſter.

Major John Young, deputy grand maſter.

1751. *James lord Boyd*, grand maſter.

Colonel John Young, deputy grand maſter.

1752. *George Drummond*, Eſq; grand maſter.

Charles Hamilton-Gordon, Eſq; deputy grand maſter.

1753. *Charles Hamilton-Gordon*, grand maſter.

Joſeph Williamſon, Eſq; deputy grand maſter.

1754. *James maſter of Forbes*, grand maſter.

David Dalrymple, Eſq; deputy grand maſter.

1755. *Sholto Charles Douglas, lord Aberdour*, grand maſter.

George

George Fraſer, Eſq; deputy grand maſter.

1756. *Sholto Charles Douglas, lord Aberdour,* grand maſter.

George Fraſer, Eſq; deputy grand maſter.

1757 *Alexander earl of Galloway,* grand maſter.

George Fraſer, Eſq; deputy grand maſter.

1758. *Alexander earl of Galloway,* grand maſter.

George Fraſer, Eſq; deputy grand maſter.

1759. *David earl of Leven,* grand maſter.

George Fraſer, Eſq; deputy grand maſter.

1760. *David earl of Leven,* grand maſter.

George Fraſer, Eſq; deputy grand maſter.

1761. *Charles earl of Elgin and Kincardine,* grand maſter.

1763. *Alexander Erſkine, earl of Kelly,* grand maſter.

1765. *James Stewart,* Eſquire, *Provoſt of Edinburgh,* grand maſter.

1767 *The R. H. earl of Dalhouſie,* grand maſter.

1769. *His excellency James Adolphus Oughton, Major General of the forces in Scotland,* grand maſter.

The *ſpirit, dignity,* and *decorum* with which the *craft* is conducted in our ſiſter-kingdom, *Scotland,* are truly great; and the *practice* of holding lodges in buildings erected *intirely* for *that* purpoſe; or, in ſpacious rooms in *private* houſes ſet apart for that uſe *ſolely,* (which univerſally prevails through the whole country) is highly commendable: muſt it not therefore give ſingular pleaſure to every *good maſon* in *this* kingdom; to find that *our* noble and worthy grand-maſter, (whoſe zeal for the dignity and proſperity of maſonry never was exceeded by any of his predeceſſors) has propoſed a plan for the laudable purpoſe of raiſing a *fund* to build a *hall*, and purchaſe jewels and furniture for the uſe of the GRAND LODGE, *independent* of the *fund* of *charity?* The reaſons produced in ſupport of this ſcheme are numerous; and, among *others*, thoſe contained in the following letter are worthy of regard; and, notwithſtanding this letter came to hand *previous* to the grand-maſter's propoſal, ſtill it may not be improper to inſert it here, as it breathes the true ſpirit of maſonry, and contains very reaſonable arguments in ſupport of this ſcheme, and alſo, as I am perſuaded that *this treatiſe* will be read by many *maſons*, who, on account of their not frequenting *lodges*, might otherwiſe remain unacquainted with ſo noble a deſign, and thereby loſe the opportunity of gratifying themſelves by contributing towards it.

To Mr. WELLINS CALCOTT,

Windſor October, 1ſt. 1768.

SIR and BROTHER,

I Underſtand we ſhall ſoon be favoured with your *maſonic* treatiſe, and ſhall eſteem my-

ſelf

ſelf obliged, if you will afford me *that* opportunity to *recall* the attention of our worthy brethren to an object which well deſerves their ſerious conſideration: I mean the erection of a commodious Building, for the particular as well as general aſſemblies of the ſociety.

A propoſal for this purpoſe was made in the reign of *Grand Maſter* FERRERS; but to whatever cauſe it then owed its miſcarriage, I beg leave to promote ſo laudable an intention, by making the *neceſſity* and *utility* of it more generally known, through the means of your publication. I therefore take my pen, as an *auxiliary* to Mr. *Edmondes*, who firſt *publiſhed* ſuch a deſign; and though I am not acquainted with that gentleman, I honour him for his *zeal*, and approve *moſt* of his ſentiments on this ſubject.

Is it not greatly to be lamented, that a *ſociety* ſo numerous, and ſo highly honoured in its members, (being in a great degree compoſed of perſons of rank and fortune) ſhould, as oft as they have occaſion for general meetings, be obliged to reſort to taverns, or to hire halls of inferior communities, and thoſe at the beſt, very ill adapted for *ſuch* meetings; as all places muſt generally be, that are not particularly conſtructed for *our* purpoſe.

Give me leave to ſay, it reflects great diſhonour on *this* country, juſtly ſtiled "the grand local ſtandard of maſonry." As Engliſhmen! we ſhould bluſh to be told, that in every *other* nation

nation in *Europe*, they hold their lodges in buildings erected and adorned for their particular uſe, and that only. I can appeal to your own experience of the *lodges* in our ſiſter kingdom, *Scotland*, for *one* inſtance; of whoſe proceedings I have oft heard you make honourable mention, particularly taking notice that they aſſembled in buildings, which were their own property, ſet a part for that purpoſe alone, whereby they not only were ſecured from every danger of moleſtation, or the inſults and diſreſpectful treatment of publicans, but accumulated *conſiderable* funds.

Beſides! our meeting at the houſes of publicans, gives us the air of a *Bacchanalian* ſociety, inſtead of that appearance of *gravity* and *wiſdom*, which our order *juſtly* requires.

How properly might it be remarked on ſuch conduct, that as almoſt all the companies that reſort with ſo much *formality* to the *city-halls*, have in view chiefly *feaſting* and *jollity*. So *maſons* aſſemble with an air of *feſtivity* at taverns, to perform the *ſerious duties* of their profeſſion, under the regulations of *morality* and *philoſophy*. Such a conduct in the eyes of every thinking man muſt appear, even on the firſt view, to be ridiculous and abſurd, and I doubt not will be thought more ſo by every one who ſhall have the peruſal of your intended treatiſe.

Some may imagine that the expence of the propoſed building (if ſuch as it really ought to be) will prove too great for the ability of the ſociety. But I fancy *many* plans might be laid down that would render it no difficult undertaking to raiſe a ſum ſufficient for the purpoſe. *One*, I will beg leave to offer for the preſent, and ſhall be very happy in finding a better propoſed and adopted.

There are at preſent under the conſtitution of *England*, near 400 lodges, ſome of which conſiſt of 60, 70, 80, and even 100 members: not including thoſe maſons, who from a variety of cauſes do not belong, as ſubſcribers, to any particular lodge; nevertheleſs retain their relation to, and reſpect for the ſociety, and who of themſelves, compoſe a very conſiderable number.

Perhaps it may be objected, there are many lodges that are not ſo numerous as what I have above ſet down; we will grant that, and take them on an average at 20 members each, which will give us the amount of 8000 maſons who attend lodges. Now I would propoſe a VOLUNTARY SUBSCRIPTION, and to promote ſo *laudable a deſign*, it would be abſurd to ſuppoſe any one would offer, *as a free gift*, leſs than five ſhillings, (many more) which will produce 2000£. No inconſiderable ſum! Yet a *trifle*, compared to what might *modeſtly* be expected from that numerous catalogue of *Princes*, *Nobles*, and other *wealthy* perſons who are of the ſociety in moſt parts of the globe, and connected with the *Engliſh* conſtitution, who would *readily* and *liberally* contribute, as ſoon

as

as a proper plan was eſtabliſhed, and application was made to them.

Nor let it be wrongly thought, beneath the dignity of our ſociety, or eſpecially the grand eſtabliſhment of it in this Kingdom, to ſolicit ſuch an aid from the *fraternity* under the *Engliſh* conſtitution in *other* countries; all maſons regularly made under the conſtitution of the *Grand Maſter* of *England*, owe allegiance to the eſtabliſhment *here*, and never fail of its protection and aſſiſtance. If therefore a ſcheme was ſettled on the above, or ſome other proper plan, there can be no doubt of effectually accompliſhing this deſireable *end*.

The *neceſſity* of ſuch a building is univerſally acknowledged through the ſociety; and a deſire of ſeeing one erected, as generally prevails. Some time ago, indeed, a ſubſcription was opened for the purpoſe of purchaſing *furniture* ſuitable for the grand lodge: but the ſtriking impropriety of procuring furniture, without *firſt* providing a place for its reception, put a ſtop at that time, to the progreſs of that affair; yet, notwithſtanding the proceeding was *then* judged premature, the ſtrongeſt aſſurances were given from every quarter of their chearful concurrence, if a proper building was *firſt* erected, to which they would *readily* contribute.

How wounding muſt it be to the *worthy* maſon, acting under the authority of *our* grand maſter,

ter, to consider the accounts we daily receive from *travelling* brethren of the magnificence of the *grand lodges abroad*, whilst *that* in *England*, which in many respects is intituled to a preference in *dignity* of all others, is destitute of a building, their own, of any sort. But, not to rest it on these *general* accounts, permit me here to send you a particular description of the *banquetting* room belonging to the lodge of *St. John* at *Marseilles*; and from the magnificence and splendour of *that* room, to which they only *retire for refreshment*, may be formed some idea of the superior excellence of the *lodge room*.

I am convinced, Sir, the *intention* with which I give you this trouble, being an humble attempt to promote the honour and advantage of the society, will be a sufficient apology, with you, for desiring you will lay the foregoing sentiments before your numerous subscribers, who I earnestly hope will think seriously on the business alluded to, and, by a noble exertion of their generosity, snatch the glorious opportunity, whilst we have the princes of the earth for our nursing fathers, and a nobleman of distinguished virtue, our *zealous* MOST WORSHIPFUL GRAND MASTER, that it may be recorded to the honour of our country and ourselves; by the *voluntary* subscription of the FREE AND ACCEPTED MASONS, in *our* day this much wanted structure was erected, for *the acquisition of knowledge of the arts and sciences, and the cultivation of moral and social virtue.*

I am, SIR, your affectionate brother,

JAMES GALLOWAY, P.M.

A DESCRIPTION *of the* Banquetting-Hall *of the* Lodge *at* Marseilles, *intituled, the* Lodge *of* St. JOHN.

At the bottom of the hall, under a gilded canopy, the valences whereof are blue, fringed with gold, is a painting, which represents the genius of masonry supporting the portrait of the king of *France*, upon a pedestal, under which there is this inscription.

Dilectissimo rege Monumentum
Amoris
Latomi. Massilienses.

A genius seated below the pedestal, presents with one hand this inscription, and with the other the arms of the lodge, with their motto.

Deo regi et Patriæ fidelitas.

Above this is a genius which crowns the king.

To the right of this painting is placed another, representing the wisdom of SOLOMON, with this inscription above it,

Prudentia.

To

To the left is another, repreſenting the courage of *St. John* the Baptiſt in remonſtrating with HEROD upon his debaucheries. The inſcription above it is,

Fortitudo.

The right ſide of the hall is ornamented with paintings of equal grandeur.

The *firſt* repreſents JOSEPH acknowledging his brethren, and pardoning them for the ill uſage he had received from them, with this inſcription,

Venia.

The *ſecond* repreſents JOB upon the dunghill, his houſe deſtroyed, his fields laid waſte by ſtorm, his wife inſulting him, and himſelf calm, lifting his hands towards heaven, with this inſcription,

Patientia.

The *third* repreſents St. PAUL and St. BARNABAS, refuſing divine honours at *Lyſtra*, with this inſcription,

Humilitas.

The *fourth*, JONATHAN, when he warned DAVID to keep from the city, in order to avoid the danger which threatned his days, with this inſcription,

Amicitia.

The *fifth*, SOLOMON ſurveying the works of the *temple*, and giving his orders for the execution

R 2 of

of the plan, which his father DAVID had left him of it, with this inſcription,

Pietas.

The *ſixth*, the charity of the *Samaritan*, with this inſcription,

Charitas.

The *ſeventh*, St. PETER and the other apoſtles paying tribute to CÆSAR, by means of the piece of money found miraculouſly in the belly of a fiſh, with this inſcription,

Fidelitas.

The left ſide of the hall contains three paintings.

The *firſt*, TOBIAS curing his father, with theſe words for the inſcription,

Filiale Debitum.

The *ſecond*, the father of the prodigal ſon, when he embraces him, and pardons his offences, with this inſcription,

Paternus Amor.

The *third* repreſents the ſacrifice of ABRAHAM, with this inſcription,

Obedientia.

On each ſide the door are two paintings of equal grandeur.

One repreſents the apoſtles giving alms in common, the inſcription,

Eleemoſyna.

The

The *other* repreſents LOT, receiving the angels into his houſe, believing them to be ſtrangers; the inſcription is,

Hoſpitalitas.

The *four* corners of the hall are decorated with four *allegorical* pictures.

In *one* are repreſented two geniuſes holding a large medal, in which are painted three pillars of a gold colour, with this motto,

Hic poſuere Locum, Virtus, Sapientia, forma.

In *another*, two geniuſes equally ſupporting a large medal, on which are repreſented three hearts ſet on fire by the ſame flame, united by the bond of the order, with this motto,

Pectora jungit Amor, Pietas que ligavit Amantes.

The two *others* are in the ſame taſte, but ſupported by one genius only, being a ſmaller ſize. The medals repreſent,

The *firſt*, three branches, one of *olive*, another of *laurel*, and another of *myrtle*, with this motto,

Hic pacem mutuo damus accipimuſque viciſſim.

The *other* a level in a hand coming from heaven, placed perpendicularly upon a heap of ſtones of unequal forms and ſizes, with this motto,

Equa lege ſortitur inſignes et imos.

ALL theſe paintings are upon a line; thoſe which are placed oppoſite the windows are intirely in front. Over the inner door of entrance is this

this inſcription, in a painting which is diſplayed by a child,

S. T. O. T. A.

Varia hæc Virtutum Exempla Fraternæ Liberalitatis Monumenta D. V. & C. Latomi Maſſilienſes, Fratribus quæ aſſequenda prebent, anno Lucis 5765.

The letters S. T. O. T. A. ſignify,

Supremo Totius Orbis Terrarum Architecto.

Each painting bears below it, the arms and blazon of the brethren who cauſed them to be painted.

Every ſpace, from one column to another, forms an intercolumniation. Upon the middle of each pilaſter, being twenty-four in number, are raiſed corbals in form of antique *Guaines*, upon which are placed the buſts of great and virtuous men of Antiquity.

The curtains to the gilded canopy are in the *Italian* taſte, and are *four* in number.

Three great branches of chryſtal light this hall at proper times, and ſerve as an additional ornament.

This hall will contain ſixty brethren, without making uſe of the *inſide* of the horſe-ſhoe table.

There are, *moreover*, two grand deſert buffets, which take up a great ſpace in the length.

FROM

FROM the foregoing *letter* and *deſcription*, I ſhall take occaſion to conſider the *temples* of the *ancients*, their ſituation, form, &c. the peruſal of which, I flatter myſelf, will afford both entertainment and *inſtruction* to the *intelligent maſon*.

The *firſt generations* of men had neither temples nor ſtatues for their gods, but worſhiped towards heaven in the open air.

The *Perſians*, even in ages when temples were common in all other countries, *not thinking the gods to be of human ſhape, as did the Greeks*, had no temples; they thought it abſurd to confine the gods within walls, "whoſe houſe and temple was this whole world," to uſe the words of CICERO.

The *Greeks*, and moſt other nations, worſhiped their gods on the tops of *high mountains*. STRABO obſerves, that the *Perſians* had neither *images* nor *altars*, but only ſacrificed to the gods on ſome *high place*.

The nations which lived near *Judea*, ſacrificed alſo on the tops of mountains. BALAK, king of *Moab*, carried BALAAM to the top of *Babal*, and other mountains, to ſacrifice to the gods, and curſe *Iſrael* from thence. The ſame cuſtom is atteſted in almoſt innumerable places of the ſacred ſcriptures; I ſhall only add the following teſtimonies, whence the *antiquity* of this cuſtom will appear. ABRAHAM was commanded by God

God to offer ISAAC his ſon for a burnt-offering upon * *one* of the mountains in the land of *Moriah*; on which mountain DAVID afterwards erected an *altar*, and by ſacrifice and prayer appeaſed the peſtilence.

And on the *ſame* mountain, (mount *Moriah*) SOLOMON, by GOD's appointment, erected a *temple*, according to the model of the *tabernacle*, which MOSES, by divine inſtruction, built in the wilderneſs. In ſucceeding ages the *temples* were often built on the *ſummits* of *mountains*. Thus it is obſerved of the *Trojan* temples, in which HECTOR is ſuppoſed to have ſacrificed. And both at *Athens* and *Rome* the moſt ſacred temples ſtood in the moſt *eminent* parts of the city.

The *temples* of the ancients were built and adorned with all poſſible ſplendour and magnificence; no pains, no charges were ſpared upon them; this they did, partly out of the great reſpect they had for the GODS, to whom they thought nothing more acceptable, and, partly

* There were in the ſame tract of ground *three* hills, *Sion*, *Moriah*, and mount *Calvary*. On *Sion* was the city and caſtle of DAVID; on *Moriah* was the *temple*; and, on mount *Calvary* CHRIST was crucified. But *all* theſe three were generally called by the name of *Sion*; whence it is, that though the *temple* was built on *Moriah*, ſcripture ſpeaks of it commonly as if it were upon mount *Sion*.

that

that they might create a reverence of the *deities*, in thoſe who came to pay their devotions there. (Vide D. POTTER's *Antiq.* of *Greece*, vol. I. and his comment upon *Lycophron*, *ad. vers.* 42.

As to the FORM of theſe ancient ſtructures, they were built after that manner, which was thought moſt agreeable to the gods to whom they were deſigned to be dedicated: For as trees, birds, and other animals were eſteemed ſacred to particular deities, ſo almoſt every god had a form of *building* peculiar to himſelf, and which they imagined more acceptable to him than any other. For inſtance, the DORICK pillars were ſacred to *Jupiter*, *Mars*, and *Hercules*: The IONICK to *Bacchus*, *Apollo*, and *Diana*: The CORINTHIAN to *Veſta* the virgin. It muſt be admitted that ſometimes *all* theſe were made uſe of in the *ſame temple*; but this was either in thoſe temples which were ſacred to *more* gods than one, or to ſome of thoſe gods who were thought to preſide over *ſeveral* things; for the ancients believing that the world was governed by divine providence, aſcribed the management of every particular affair to this or that *deity*: Thus MARS was thought to preſide over *war*; VENUS over *love*; ſo MERCURY was the god of *merchants*, *orators*, and *thieves*; MINERVA was the goddeſs of *warriors*, *ſcholars*, *artificers*, &c. Therefore, it is no wonder that in *ſome* of the temples dedicated to *her*, there were *three* rows

S of

of *pillars*; the firſt of the DORICK, the ſecond of the CORINTHIAN, the third of the IONICK order.

With reſpect to the SITUATION of their temples, VITRUVIUS informs us, Wherever they ſtood, if the place would permit, it was contrived, that the windows being open, they might receive the rays of the riſing ſun, (lib. VI. c. 5.) The *frontiſpiece* placed *towards* the *weſt*, and the *altars* and *ſtatues* towards the *eaſt*; ſo that they who came to worſhip might have their faces towards *them*, becauſe it was an ancient cuſtom of the *heathens* to worſhip with their faces towards the *eaſt*. This is affirmed by CLEMENS *of Alexandria*, (Strom. VIII.) and HYGINUS, the *freed-man of* AUGUSTUS CÆSAR, (*De agrorum limit. Conſ.* lib. I.) to have been the moſt ancient ſituation of temples; and that the placing the *front* of temples towards the *eaſt* was only a device of latter ages. Nevertheleſs, the way of building temples towards the *eaſt*, ſo as the doors being opened ſhould receive the rays of the riſing ſun, was very ancient; (DION. THRAX.) and in later ages almoſt univerſal; moſt of the temples were then ſo contrived, that the entrance and ſtatues ſhould look towards the *eaſt*, and they who paid their devotion towards the *weſt*, as we are expreſsly told by PORPHYRY, (*libro de Antro Nympharum.*) In the ſame manner the *eaſtern* nations commonly built *their* tem-

temples, as appears from the temples of the *Syrian goddeſs* in LUCIAN. The temple of *Memphis*, built by PSAMMENICUS, king of *Egypt*, in DIODORUS *the Sycilian.* That of *Vulcan* erected by another *Egyptian* king. (HERODOTUS, lib. II. &c.)

HENCE it appears, that the reaſon why the *heathens* erected their temples *eaſt* and *weſt*, was to receive the rays of the riſing ſun, which *planet* many of *thoſe* nations were accuſtomed to worſhip.

And we find the *tabernacle*, erected in the wilderneſs, and the *temple* at *Jeruſalem*, as alſo moſt places of divine adoration in the preſent age, to be ſituated in the *ſame manner*, but *not* for the *ſame reaſon* : for we read that the *Jews* were forbid to worſhip with their faces towards the *eaſt* : Accordingly, the *temple* had no avenue to it but *from* the *eaſt*. So that in their *approach* to the temple, and during the time of their *adoration* therein, they had their faces towards the *weſt*, and their backs to the *riſing ſun* ; which was done, according to the opinion of the beſt commentators, to prevent the people from worſhipping the *ſun and hoſt of heaven*, a ſpecies of idolatry they were very prone to. And as they were by this means to be prevented from falling into that mode of idolatry in their worſhip, conſequently the *reaſon* for ſituating the *tabernacle*, and (after that example) the *temple* could not be the *ſame* which influenced the *heathens* in the ſituation of *their* temples. Therefore, we may reaſonably account for *their* ſituation, by ſuppoſing that when the *tabernacle* was erected, Moses, purſuing the practice of the *Egyptians*, who always inculcated their religious documents by means of *allegory* and *ſymbol*, foreſeeing the difficulties which he would have to encounter before he ſhould arrive in the promiſed land, and having already experienced the inſtability of the *Iſraëlites*, cauſed the *tabernacle* to be erected *eaſt* and *weſt*, to excite in *them* a firm reliance on the *omnipotence* of that GOD, who had then lately wrought ſo great a miracle in their favour, by cauſing a *wind* to blow firſt *eaſt* and then *weſt*, whereby *they* ſafely eſcaped from the *Egyptians* upon dry land, even through the midſt of *a ſea*, which nevertheleſs overwhelmed and totally deſtroyed their purſuers. And as they were liable to meet with many diſtreſſes in their ſojournment in the *wilderneſs*, ſo, as oft as they ſhould behold the *ſituation* of the tabernacle, their *faith* might be ſtrengthened, and by a firm reliance on ALMIGHTY GOD, they might be enabled to proceed with reſolution and chearfulneſs.

And as the *tabernacle* was at *that time* to be a conſtant exhortation to *them*, from that great inſtance of *Omnipotence*, to confide in GOD under all their embarraſſments, ſo, the *temple*, afterwards built by Solomon, in the *ſame form and*

ſitu-

ſituation, was to be a *laſting* monument to their *poſterity*, of the mighty works the LORD had performed in conducting their *fore-fathers* out of their captivity into the promiſed land. And *this* alſo may be deemed a very ſufficient reaſon, why places for *Chriſtian* worſhip, after the pattern of the ſaid *tabernacle* and *temple*, have ever been, and ſtill are, generally erected in the *ſame* manner; for as *human* creatures *we*, as well as our *fore-fathers*, ſtand in need to be *continually* reminded of our *weakneſs*, and a neceſſary conſtant dependance, on an *omnipotent* and *all-gracious* BEING.

THE
DUTIES
OF A
FREE-MASON,
IN
SEVERAL CHARGES,
DELIVERED

In *regular* LODGES, held under the Constitution of the GRAND-MASTER of *ENGLAND*.

Honour all men. Love the Brother-hood. Fear God. Honour the King.

1 PET. ii. v. 17.

A CHARGE, *delivered to the Members of the* Lodge *of* FREE and ACCEPTED MASONS, *held at the* Castle-inn, MARLBOROUGH, *at a Meeting for the Distribution of* CHARITY *to twenty-four poor People, at which most of the* LADIES *in* Marlborough *were present, Sept.* 11, *A. L.* 5769.

By *THOMAS DUNCKERLY*, Esq; Right Worshipful Provincial Grand Master over the LODGES in *Hampshire*, and Right Worshipful Master of *that* LODGE.

Blessed is he that considereth the POOR.

Psalm xli. v. 1.

BRETHREN,

IT is with the greatest satisfaction I meet you here in the cause of *charity*: *Charity* is the basis of *our* order; it is for this purpose we have a Grand Lodge at *London*, another at *Edinburgh*, and a third at *Dublin*. Lodges are now held on every part of this globe, and charities are collected and ſent to the reſpective *grand* lodge of each kingdom or ſtate: *there* the diſtreſt brethren apply and find relief: nor is any exception made to difference of country or religion.

For, as in the ſight of God we are all equally his children, having the ſame common parent and preſerver—ſo we, in like manner, look on *every* free-maſon as our brother; nor regard where he was born or educated, provided he is a good man, an honeſt man, which is "the nobleſt work of God."

A laudable cuſtom prevailed among our ancient brethren; after they had ſent their donations to the *general* charities, they conſidered the diſtreſſes of thoſe in *particular* that reſided in their reſpective neighbourhoods, and aſſiſted them with ſuch a ſum as could be conveniently ſpared from the *lodge*. In humble imitation of this maſonic principle, I recommend the preſent charity to your conſideration; to which you readily and unanimouſly conſented. The ſum is, indeed, but ſmall: yet, when it is conſidered that this lodge is in its infant ſtate; having been conſtituted little more than three months: I hope, as the widow's mite was acceptable, *this* act of ours will be conſidered, not with reſpect to the ſum, but the principles by which we are influenced.

I have told you in the *lodge*, and I repeat it now, that *brotherly-love*, *relief*, and *truth*, are the

the grand principles of maſonry, and as the principal part of the company are unacquainted with the original intention of this ſociety, it may be proper for their information, and your inſtruction, that I explain thoſe principles, by which it is our duty in particular to be actuated.

By *Brotherly-love*, we are to underſtand that generous principle of the ſoul, which reſpects the human ſpecies as one family, created by an all-wiſe Being, and placed on this globe for the mutual aſſiſtance of each other.—It is this attractive *principle*, or power, that draws men together and unites them in bodies politic, families, ſocieties, and the various orders and denominations among men. But as moſt of theſe are partial, contracted or confined to a particular country, religion, or opinion; *our* order, on the contrary, is calculated to unite mankind as one family: High and low, rich and poor, one with another; to adore the ſame God, and obſerve his law. All worthy members of this ſociety are free to viſit every lodge in the world; and though he knows not the language of the country, yet by a ſilent univerſal language of our own, he will gain admittance, and find that *true* friendſhip, which flows from the brotherly-love I am now deſcribing.

At that peaceable and harmonious meeting he will hear no *diſputes* concerning religion or politics; no *ſwearing*; no *obſcene*, *immoral*, or *ludicrous* diſcourſe; no other contention but *who can work beſt, who can agree beſt.*

To ſubdue our paſſions, and improve in uſeful ſcientific knowledge; to inſtruct the younger brethren, and initiate the unenlightened, are principal duties in the lodge: which, when done, and the word of God is cloſed, we indulge with the ſong and chearful glaſs, ſtill obſerving the ſame decency and regularity, with ſtrict attention to the golden mean, believing with the poet, that

God is paid when man receives,
T' enjoy is to obey.

Let me travel from *eaſt* to *weſt*, or between *north* and *ſouth*, when I meet a *true* brother I ſhall find a friend, who will do all in his power to ſerve me, without having the leaſt view of ſelf-intereſt: and if I am poor and in diſtreſs, he will relieve me to the utmoſt of his power, intereſt, and capacity. This is the ſecond grand principle: for, *relief* will follow where there is brotherly-love.

I have already mentioned our general charities as they are at preſent conducted; it remains now that I conſider particular donations given from private lodges, either to thoſe that are not maſons, or to a brother in diſtreſs. And firſt, with reſpect to a charity like this before us; perhaps it is better to be diſtributed in ſmall ſums, that more may receive the benefit, than to give

it

it in larger ſums, which would confine it to few.

With regard to a brother in diſtreſs, who ſhould happen to apply to this *lodge*, or any *particular* member for relief, it is neceſſary that I inform you in what manner you are to receive *him*. And here I cannot help regretting, that ſuch is the depravity of the human heart, there is no religion or ſociety free from bad profeſſors, or unworthy members, for as it is impoſſible for us to read the heart of man, the beſt regulated ſocieties may be impoſed on, by the inſinuations of the artful, and hypocriſy of the abandoned. It ſhould therefore by no means leſſen the dignity and excellency of the *royal craft*, becauſe it is our misfortune to have bad men among us, any more than the purity and holineſs of the *Chriſtian* religion ſhould be doubted, becauſe too many of the wicked and profligate approach the holy altar.

Since, therefore, theſe things are ſo: be careful whenever a brother applies for relief, to examine ſtrictly whether he is worthy of acceptance: enquire the *cauſe* of his misfortunes, and if you are ſatisfied they are not the reſult of *vice* or *extravagance*, relieve him with ſuch a ſum as the lodge ſhall think proper, and aſſiſt him with your intereſt and recommendation, that he may be employed according to his capacity, and not *eat the bread of idleneſs*. This will be acting conſiſtent

ſiſtent with TRUTH, which is the *third* grand principle of maſonry.

TTUTH is a divine attribute, and the foundation of all maſonic virtues: to be *good men* and *true*, is part of the firſt great leſſon we are taught; and at the commencement of our freedom, we are exhorted to be fervent and zealous in the practice of *truth* and *goodneſs*. It is not ſufficient that we walk in the light, unleſs we do the *truth*. All hypocriſy and deceit muſt be baniſhed from us—Sincerity and plain dealing compleat the harmony of the brethren, within and without the lodge; and will render us acceptable in the ſight of that great Being, *unto whom all hearts are open, all deſires known, and from whom no ſecrets are hid*. There is a charm in *truth* that draws and attracts the mind continually towards it: the more we diſcover, the more we deſire, and the great reward is, *wiſdom*, *virtue*, and *happineſs*. This is an edifice founded upon a rock, which malice cannot ſhake, or time deſtroy, What a ſecret ſatisfaction do we enjoy, when in ſearching for truth, we find the *firſt principles* of uſeful ſcience, ſtill preſerved among us, as we received them, by *oral* tradition from the earlieſt ages; and we alſo find this truth corroborated by the teſtimonies of the beſt and greateſt men the world has produced. But this is not all; the *ſacred* writings confirm what I aſſert; the ſublime part of our ancient myſtery being

being there to be found; nor can any *Christian* brother be a *good* mason that does not make the word of *God* his first and principal study.

I sincerely congratulate you on the happy establishment of this lodge, and the prospect you have of its utility and permanency, by the choice you have made of members capable to conduct it. Let wisdom direct you to contrive for the best.—Strengthen the cause of masonry, by mutual friendship, which is the companion and support of fraternal love, and which will never suffer any misunderstanding to inflame a brother, or cause him to behave unbecoming a member of our peaceable and harmonious society. Let us then resolve to beautify and adorn our order, by discharging the duties of our respective stations, as good subjects, good parents, good husbands, good masters, and dutiful children; for by so doing, we shall put to silence the reproaches of foolish men. As you know these things, brethren, happy are ye if ye do them; and thrice happy shall I esteem it to be looked on as the founder of a society in *Marlborough* whose grand principles are, brotherly-love, relief, and truth.

Let us consider these poor persons as our brothers and sisters, and be thankful to Almighty God, that he has been pleased to make us his instruments of affording them this small relief; most humbly supplicating the GRAND ARCHITECT OF THE UNIVERSE, *from whom all holy desires, all good counsels, and all just works do proceed,*

ceed, to blefs our undertaking, and grant that we may *continue* to add fome little comfort to the *poor* of this town.

Next to the *Deity*, whom can I fo properly addrefs myfelf to, as the moft beautiful part of the creation?

You have heard, *Ladies*, our grand principles explained, with the inftructions given to the brethren; and I doubt not but at other times you have heard many difrefpectful things faid of this fociety. Envy, malice, and all uncharitablenefs will never be at a lofs to decry, find fault, and raife objections to what they do not know. How great then are the obligations *you* lay on this lodge! with what fuperior efteem, refpect, and regard, are we to look on every lady prefent, that has done us the honour of her company this evening. To have the fanction of the *fair* is our higheft ambition, as our greateft care will be to preferve it. The virtues of humanity are peculiar to your fex; and we flatter ourfelves, the moft fplendid ball could not afford *you* greater pleafure, than to fee the human heart made happy, and the *poor* and *diftreft* obtain prefent *relief*.

A

A CHARGE, *delivered in* St. George's *Lodge at* TAUNTON *in the County of* SOMERSET, *on the Feaſt of* St. JOHN the Baptiſt, *A. L.* 5765, *A. D.* 1765.

By the Right Worſhipful Brother *JOHN WHITMASH, on his* reſigning *the chair.*

Worthy BRETHREN,

PROVIDENCE having placed me in ſuch a ſphere in life, as to afford me but little time for ſpeculation, I cannot pretend to have made mankind my particular ſtudy; yet, this I have obſerved, that *curioſity* is one of the moſt prevailing paſſions in the human breaſt. The mind of man is kept in a perpetual thirſt after knowledge, nor can he bear to be ignorant of what he thinks others know. Any thing *ſecret* or *new* immediately excites an uneaſy ſenſation, and becomes the proper fuel of curioſity, which will be found ſtronger or weaker in proportion to the time and opportunities that individuals have for indulging it. It is obſervable further, that when this paſſion is excited, and not inſtantly gratified, inſtead of waiting for better intelligence, and uſing the proper means of removing the darkneſs that invelops the object of it, we precipitately form ideas which are generally in the extremes. If the object promotes pleaſure or advantage, we then load it with commendations; if it appears in the oppoſite view, or if we are ignorant of it, we then *abſurdly*, as well as *diſingenuouſly*, condemn, and pretend at leaſt to deſpiſe it. This, my brethren, has been the fate of the moſt valuable inſtitution in the world, *Chriſtianity* excepted, I mean *free-maſonry*. Thoſe who are acquainted with the nature and deſign of it, cannot, *if they have good hearts*, but admire and eſpouſe it; and if thoſe who are in the *dark*, or whoſe minds are diſpoſed to *evil*, ſhould ſlight or ſpeak diſreſpectfully of it, it certainly is no *diſgrace*. When *order* ſhall produce confuſion, when *harmony* ſhall give riſe to diſcord, and *proportion* ſhall be the ſource of irregularity, then, and not till then, will *free-maſonry* be unworthy the patronage of the *great*, the *wiſe*, and *good*.

To love as brethren, to be ready to communicate, to ſpeak truth one to another, are the dictates of reaſon and revelation; and you know that they are likewiſe the foundation, the conſtituent parts of *free-maſonry*.

None,

None, therefore, who believe the divine original of the *ſacred volume*, and are influenced by a ſpirit of humanity, friendſhip, and benevolence, can with the leaſt propriety object to our ancient and venerable inſtitution.

For my own part, ever ſince I have had the honour to be enrolled in the liſt of maſons, as I knew it was my duty, ſo I have made it my buſineſs, to become acquainted with the principles on which our glorious ſuperſtructure is founded. And like the *miner*, the farther I have advanced the richer has been my diſcovery ; and the treaſure conſtantly opening to my view, has proved a full and ſatisfactory reward of all my *labours*.

Conſcious that the ſame pleaſure would attend others, in the ſame purſuits, I ſincerely wiſhed for the eſtabliſhment of a lodge *in this town :* but as wiſhes, without endeavours, are not the means of accompliſhment, I became, therefore, actively concerned for the completion of ſo valuable a deſign. And you, and only you, who are maſons *in heart*, can form the leaſt idea of the joy I felt, when, upon enquiry, I found that this neighbourhood was not deſtitute of faithful brethren ; brethren ! fired with an equal ardour for the proſperity of *maſonry*, and who with equal alacrity and pleaſure, embarked in the noble deſign, and, like true craftſmen, laboured in this long wiſh'd-for fabrick : The ſtrength of whoſe *baſis*, the beauty of whoſe *ſymmetry*, the *order* of whoſe *parts*, have rendered it the admiration of ſome, the model of others, and the delight of ourſelves.

You will therefore give me leave moſt ſincerely to congratulate the *lodge*, on the ſucceſs that has attended our united labours for the honour of the craft in *this* town, as likewiſe on the return of this feſtival, the general day of inſtalment of new officers. May we all live to celebrate repeatedly this anniverſary with increaſing felicity and honour; and may the true *maſonic* ſpirit of generoſity, kindneſs, and brotherly-love, be our laſting *cement*.

By the rules of this lodge I am now to reſign the *chair*. But I cannot do this with entire ſatisfaction, until I have teſtified the grateful ſenſe I feel of the honour I received in being advanced to it.

Your generous and unanimous choice of me for your *firſt* maſter, demands my thankful acknowledgements, though at the ſame time I ſincerely wiſh, that my abilities had been more adequate to the charge, which your kind partiality elected me to. But this has always been, and ſtill is my greateſt conſolation, that however deficient I may have been in the diſcharge of my duty, no one can boaſt *a heart* more devoted to the good of the *inſtitution* in general, and the reputation of this *lodge* in particular.

Though

Though I am apprehensive I have already trespassed on your patience, yet if I might be indulged, I would humbly lay before you a few reflections, adapted to the business of the day, which being the effusions of a heart *truly masonic*, will, it is hoped, be received with candour by you.

Every association of men, as well as this of *free-masons*, must for the sake of order and harmony, be regulated by certain laws, and for that purpose proper officers must be appointed, and empowered to carry those laws into execution, to preserve a degree of uniformity, at least to restrain any irregularity that might render such associations inconsistent. For we may as reasonably suppose an army may be duly disciplined, well provided, and properly conducted, without generals or other officers, as that a *society* can be supported without governors, and their subalterns, or (which is the same) without some *form* of *government* to answer the end of the institution, And as such an arrangement must be revered, it becomes a necessary pre-requisite that *a temper* should be discovered in the several members adapted to the respective *stations* they are to fill.

This thought will suggest to you, that those who are qualified to preside as *officers* in a *lodge*, will not be elated with that honour, but, losing sight of it, will have only in view, the *service* their

their office demands. Their reproofs will be dictated by *friendſhip*, ſoftened by *candour*, and enforced with *mildneſs* and *affection*; in the whole of their deportment they will preſerve a degree of *dignity* tempered with *affability* and *eaſe*. This conduct, while it endears them to others, will not fail to raiſe their own reputation, and as *envy* ſhould not be ſo much as once named among *free-maſons*, it will effectually prevent the growth of it, ſhould it unfortunately ever appear.

Such is the nature of our conſtitution, that as ſome muſt of neceſſity, *rule* and *teach*, ſo others muſt of courſe learn to *obey*; humility therefore in *both* becomes an *eſſential duty*, for pride and ambition, like a worm at the root of the tree, will prey on the vitals of our *peace*, *harmony*, and *brotherly-love*.

Had not this excellent temper prevailed, when the foundation of SOLOMON's temple was firſt laid, it is eaſy to ſee, that *glorious* edifice would never have roſe to a height of ſplendour, which aſtoniſhed the world.

Had *all* employed in this work been maſters, or ſuperintendants, who muſt have prepared the timber in the foreſt, or hewn the ſtone in the quarry? Yet though they were numbered and claſſed under different denominations, as princes, rulers, provoſts, comforters of the people, ſtone-

quarers,

quarers, ſculptors, &c. ſuch was their unanimity, that they ſeemed actuated by *one* ſpirit, influenced by *one* principle.

Merit alone then intituled to preferment; an indiſputable inſtance of which we have in the *deputy-grand-maſter* of that great undertaking, who, without either wealth or power, without any other diſtinction, than that of being the *widow's ſon*, was appointed by the grand-maſter and approved by the people for this ſingle reaſon, becauſe he was a *ſkilful* artificer.

Let theſe conſiderations, my worthy brethren, animate *us* in the purſuits of ſo noble a ſcience, that we may all be qualified to fill, in rotation, the moſt diſtinguiſhed places in the lodge, and keep the *honours* of the craft, (which are the juſt rewards of our labour) in a regular circulation.

And as none are leſs qualified to *govern*, than thoſe, who have not learnt to *obey*, permit me in the warmeſt manner to recommend to you all a conſtant attendance in *this* place, a due *obedience* to the *laws* of *our inſtitution*, and a reſpectful ſubmiſſion to the *directions* of your officers, that you may prove to mankind the propriety of your election, and ſecure the eſtabliſhment of this ſociety to lateſt poſterity.

An

An ADDRESS *to the* Lodge *of* Perfect Friendſhip, *held at the* Shakeſpear and Greyhound Inn *and* Tavern *at* Bath, *on the Feſtival of St.* John the Evangeliſt, *A. L.* 5768, *A. D.* 1768.

By Brother *J. S. GAUDRY*,

The Right Worſhipful Brother WILLIAM BROWNE, Maſter, in the Chair.

Worthy BRETHREN,

THIS Lodge is ſo juſtly renowned for its excellent *plan* and *proceedings*, that exhortations to a more punctual diſcharge of your reſpective duties, would appear both unneceſſary and vain. Still, permit me, without taking offence, to make a few trite obſervations on the *nature of our inſtitution*, for the benefit of ſuch *newly* admitted brethren, as may at this time be preſent.

Would every brother conſider the advantages he derives, as a *man*, by being a *free-maſon*, he would readily confeſs, that the glorious precepts inculcated in all regular lodges, are calculated in the

moſt

moſt eſpecial manner to faſhion the mind to goodneſs. In *them* it is ſtrongly recommended to us, to cultivate our ſeveral duties to God, our neighbour, and ourſelves. To have *faith* in God, *hope* in ſalvation, and *charity* for all mankind; and yet it muſt be confeſſed there are *ſome*, who have been initiated *maſons*, and who, to their eternal *ſhame*, not only diſregard our excellent documents, but, to all *appearance*, are little inclined to regulate their conduct by them, any longer than they are conſtrained to do it in a lodge; when, alas! the qualifications of a *good maſon* would decorate the crown of the greateſt monarch.

As the rules of this fraternity have a direct tendency to promote *moral* and *ſocial* virtue, let *us* carefully baniſh from our breaſts every inclination, and avoid every practice, that might obſtruct this noble intention, ever being diſpoſed to humane and friendly offices, and particularly to relieve the diſtreſſes of indigent brethren. The royal *Pſalmiſt* ſays, in raptures, *the bleſſing of him that was ready to periſh came upon me, and I cauſed the widow's heart to ſing for joy.* May *we* therefore rejoice in every opportunity of ſerving and obliging each other, for in *ſuch* exerciſes we anſwer one principal end of our inſtitution.

It is, and ſhould be, the glory of every member of *this* lodge, that our well regulated conduct has engaged us the eſteem of every brother who has done us the honour of a viſit. Surely then we ought never to be wanting in a chearful performance of thoſe duties which are ſo conducive to the *eſtabliſhing* that good name, which we have endeavoured to merit.

For this laudable purpoſe let me obſerve, that a due attendance at the lodge becomes abſolutely requiſite: For, by frequently aſſembling together we ſhall harmonize in ſentiments, and grow in affection; and thus become ſufficiently guarded againſt the diſagreeable effects naturally reſulting from a *roughneſs* of behaviour, a *contemptuous* carriage, a *cenſorious* diſpoſition, or a *contradicting* temper, and unity, peace, and pleaſure, will preſide. Theſe will be the happy effects of a *due* attendance on the lodge, and how far *that* is the *duty*, as well as the *intereſt*, of every member, *regularly* admitted, his own heart can ſufficiently tell him; his *engagements* on his initiation were not ſo *inſignificant* as to be readily forgot, and when *duly* conſidered will, I hope, appear too *important* to be *trifled* with, for, The *Great Architect of the Univerſe* is our *ſupreme Grand maſter*, and He is—*a ſearcher of hearts.*

In the next place permit me, worthy brethren, to remind you of that veneration and obedience, which

which is due to the particular officers in the lodge in their refpective ftations. *You* well know that the *internal*, and not the *external*, qualifications of a man, are what *mafonry* regards, when he is admitted a member. Let us then be careful to juftify ourfelves by a behaviour; to *fuperiors*, fubmiflive; to *equals*, courteous and affable; to *inferiors*, kind and condefcending.

MASONRY is the daughter of Heaven! The Patronefs of the *liberal arts* and *fciences*, which polifh and adorn human nature: *thankful* ought they to be who have it in their power to embrace her, and *happy* are thofe who do. SHE teaches the way to content, with fervency and zeal unfeigned, as fure of being unchangeable as of ending in felicity.

Invefted as we are with that ancient and noble *badge*, which yields preference to no honour or order in the univerfe, let us determine to abhor every act that may leffen the dignity of our profeffion, which to this hour is the glory of the greateft men on the face of the globe. Let us conform our whole lives to that *great Light*, the Law of God, and let our actions convince the world, that truth, brotherly-love, and a defire to afford relief to the diftreffed, are the grand Principles whereon we proceed. So that this life having paffed in the difcharge of our duties as *men* and *free-maſons*, we may at length be received into the preſence of our SUPREME GRAND-MASTER and rejoice in hearing him ſay, *Well done ye good and faithful ſervants, enter ye into the joy of your LORD.*

A Short CHARGE, *delivered to* Brother WILLIAM WINSTON, *on his being invested and installed* Right Worshipful Master of the PALLADIAN Lodge *of* Free and accepted Masons, *in the* CITY *of* HEREFORD, *on the Festival of* St. JOHN the Evangelist, *A. L.* 5767, *A. D.* 1767.

By Bro. *WELLINS CALCOTT*, P. M.

Right Worshipful SIR,

BY the unanimous voice of the members of this lodge, you are elected to the mastership thereof for the ensuing half-year; and I have the happiness of being deputed to invest you with this ensign of your office; be it ever in your thoughts, that the ancients particularly held this *symbol* to be a just, a striking *emblem* of the *divinity*. They said, the GODS, who are the authors of every thing established in *wisdom*, *strength*, and *beauty*, were properly represented by *this* figure *. May you, worthy brother, not only consider it as a mark of honour in this assembly, but also, let it ever remind you of your duty both to God and MAN. And as you profess the *sacred volume* to be your *spiritual tressel* board, may you make it your particular care to square your life and conversation according to the rules and designs laid down therein.

You have been of too long standing, and are too good a member of our community, to require *now* any information in the duty of your office. What you have seen *praise-worthy* in others, we doubt not you will *imitate*; and what you have seen *defective*, you will in yourself *amend*.

We have therefore the greatest reason to expect you will be constant and regular in your attendance on the lodge, faithful and diligent in the discharge of your duty: and that you will make the honour of the *supreme architect of the universe*, and the good of the *craft*, chief objects of your regard.

We likewise trust you will pay a punctual attention to the laws and regulations of this *society*, as more particularly becoming your present station; and that you will at the same time require a due obedience to them, from every other member, well knowing that without *this* the best of laws become useless.

* Vide Proclus in EUCLID, Lib. XI. Def. 2 and 34.

For

For a pattern of imitation, conſider the great luminary of nature, which, riſing in the *eaſt*, regularly diffuſes light and luſtre to all within its circle. In like manner it is your province, with due decorum, to ſpread and communicate light and inſtruction to the brethren in the lodge.

From the knowledge we already have of your zeal and abilities, we reſt aſſured you will diſcharge the duties of this important ſtation in ſuch a manner, as will greatly redound to the honour of yourſelf, as well as of thoſe members over whom you are elected to preſide.

An

An ADDRESS *to the ſame* LODGE,

By Brother *W. CALCOTT*,

Immediately after the Inveſtiture *and* Inſtalment *of the reſt of the* OFFICERS.

Worthy BRETHREN,

I Flatter myſelf there is no *maſon* of my acquaintance inſenſible of the ſincere regard I ever had, and hope ever to retain, for our venerable inſtitution; certain I am, if this eſtabliſhment ſhould ever be held in little eſteem by the members, it muſt be owing to the want of a due ſenſe of the excellence of its principles, and the *ſalutary* laws and *ſocial* duties on which it is founded.

But ſometimes mere curioſity, views of ſelf-intereſt, or a groundleſs preſumption, that the *principal* buſineſs of a lodge is mirth and entertainment, hath induced men of looſe principles and diſcordant tempers to procure admiſſion into our

our community, *this* together with an unpardonable inattention of those who proposed them, to their lives and conversations have constantly occasioned great discredit and uneasiness to the *craft*, such persons being no ways qualified for a society *founded* upon wisdom, and *cemented* by *morality* and *Christian-love*.

Therefore let it be *your* peculiar care to pay strict attention to the merit and character of those, who, from among the circle of your acquaintance, may be desirous of becoming members of our society, lest through your inadvertency, the unworthy part of mankind should find means to introduce themselves among you, whereby you will *discourage* the reputable and worthy.

Self-love is a reigning principle in all men; and there is not a more effectual method of ingratiating ourselves with each other, than by mutual complaisance and respect; by agreement (with each other) in judgment and practice. *This* makes *society* pleasing, and *friendship* durable; *which* can *never* be the case, when mens principles and dispositions are opposite, and not adapted for *unity*. We must be moved by the same *passions*, governed by the same *inclinations*, and moulded by the same *morals*, before we can please or be pleased in *society*. No *community* or *place* can make a man happy, who is not furnished with a temper of mind to relish felicity. The *wise* and *royal grand master* SOLOMON tells us, and experience confirms it, that, " the *light* is ſweet, and a pleaſant thing it is to behold the *ſun.*" Yet for this pleaſure we are wholly indebted to that aſtoniſhing piece of heavenly workmanſhip, the *eye*, and the ſeveral organs of ſight. Let the *eye* be diſtempered, and all objects, which though *they* remain the ſame in themſelves, to *us* loſe their beauty and luſtre, let the *eye* be *totally* deſtroyed, *then* the ſenſe which depends upon it, is *loſt* alſo, and the whole body is full of darkneſs. So it is with that *maſon*, who has not a frame and temper of mind adapted to our inſtitution, without which the blended allurements of pleaſure and inſtruction to be found in a lodge, muſt become taſteleſs, and of none effect. Likewiſe let his *conduct* and *circumſtances* in life be ſuch, as may not have the leaſt tendency to diminiſh the *credit* of the ſociety: and be ye ever diſpoſed to honour *good men* for their virtues, and *wiſe men* for their knowledge: Good men for propagating virtue and religion all over the world, and wiſe men for encouraging arts and ſciences, and diffuſing them from eaſt to weſt, and between north and ſouth, rejecting all who are not of *good repute*, *ſound morals*, and *competent underſtandings*. Hence you will derive honour and happineſs to yourſelves, and drink deeply of thoſe ſtreams of felicity, which the unenlightened never can be indulged with a taſte of.

For by theſe means exceſs and irregularity muſt be ſtrangers within your walls. On *ſobriety* your pleaſure depends, on *regularity* your reputation, and not *your* reputation only, but the reputation of the *whole* body.

Theſe *general* cautions, if duly attended to, will continually evince your wiſdom by their effects, for I can with confidence aver from experience, that nothing more contributes to the *diſſolutions* of a lodge, than too great a number of members * indiſcriminately made; want of regulation in their expences, and keeping unſeaſonable hours.

To guard againſt this fatal conſequence we ſhall do well to cultivate the following virtues, viz. *prudence*, *temperance*, and *frugality*. Virtues which are the beſt and propereſt ſupports of every community.

Prudence is the queen and guide of all other virtues, the ornament of our actions, the *ſquare* and *rule* of our affairs. It is the knowledge and choice of thoſe things we muſt either approve

---

* It would be as abſurd to imagine, that happineſs is found in a *numerous* lodge, where the members are indiſcriminately admitted, as to think that true greatneſs conſiſts in ſize and dimenſions; for as Mr. *Pope* obſerves, " Let an edifice be ever ſo vaſt, unleſs the parts relate to each other in *harmony*, the *monſtrous whole* will be but a cluſter of *littleneſſes* unnaturally crowded together.

or reject; and implies to consult and deliberate well, to judge and resolve well, to conduct and execute well.

Temperance consists in the government of our appetites and affections, so as to use the good things of this life as not to abuse them, either by a sordid and ungrateful parsimony on the one hand, or a profuse and prodigal indulgence to excess, on the other. *This* virtue has many powerful arguments in its favour; for, as we value our health, wealth, reputation, family, and friends, our character, as men, as Christians, as members of *society* in *general*, and as FREE-MASONS in *particular*, all conspire to call on us for the exercise of *this* virtue; in short, it comprehends a strict observance of the apostles exhortation; "Be ye temperate in all things;" not only avoiding what is in itself *improper*, but also, whatever has the least or most remote appearance of *impropriety*, that the tongue of the slanderer may be struck dumb, and malevolence disarmed of its sting.

Frugality, the natural associate of *prudence* and *temperance*, is what the meanest station necessarily calls for, the most exalted cannot dispence with. It is absolutely requisite in *all* stations: it is highly necessary to the supporting *every* desireable character, to the establishment of *every* society, to the interest of *every* individual in the community. It is a *moral*, it is a

Christian

Chriſtian virtue. It implies the ſtrict obſervation of decorum in the ſeaſons of *relaxation*, and of every *enjoyment*, and is that temper of mind which is diſpoſed to employ every acquiſition only to the glory of the giver, our own happineſs, and that of our fellow-creatures.

If we fail not in the exerciſe of *theſe* virtues (which are eſſential ſupports of every lodge of FREE and ACCEPTED MASONS) they will effectually ſecure us from thoſe unconſtitutional practices, which have proved ſo fatal to *this* ſociety. For *prudence* will diſcover the abſurdity and folly of expecting true harmony, without due attention to the choice of our members. *Temperance* will check every appearance of exceſs, and fix rational limitations to our hours of enjoyment. And *frugality* will proſcribe extravagance, and keep our expences within proper bounds.

The *Lacedemonians* had a law among them, that every one ſhould ſerve the *gods* with *as little expence* as he could, herein differing from all other *Grecians*; and LYCURGUS being aſked for what reaſon he made this inſtitution, ſo diſagreeable to the ſentiments of all other men? anſwered, Leſt at any time the ſervice of the *gods* ſhould be intermitted; for he feared, if religion ſhould be as *expenſive* there as in other parts of *Greece*, it might ſometime or other happen that the divine worſhip out of the *covetouſneſs* of ſome, and the *poverty* of others, would be *neglected*. This

ob-

obſervation will hold equally good with reſpect to *maſons*, and will, I hope, by them be properly *applied*.

I would not be underſtood here to mean, that becauſe theſe three *moral* virtues are *particularly* pointed out, as eſſentially neceſſary to the good diſcipline and ſupport of a *lodge*, nothing more is required, for *ſocial* muſt be united with *moral* excellencies; was a man to be *merely* prudent, temperate and frugal, and yet be unaccuſtomed to the duties of humanity, ſincerity, generoſity, &c. he would be at moſt but a *uſeleſs*, if not a *worthleſs* member of *ſociety*, and a much worſe *maſon*.

In the next place permit me to remind you, that a due *attendance* on the lodge for your own improvement, and the reputation of *maſonry* in general, is *abſolutely* neceſſary; for your own improvement, becauſe the advantages naturally reſulting from the *practice* of principles therein taught, are the higheſt ornament of human nature; and for the credit of the community, becauſe it is your indiſpenſible duty to ſupport ſuch a character in life as is there enjoined. The prevalency of good *example* is great, and no language is ſo expreſſive as a *conſiſtent* life and converſation; *theſe* once forfeited in the *maſonic* character, will diminiſh a man, not only in the eſteem of perſons of ſenſe, learning, and probity,

but

but even men of *inferior* qualities will ſeldom fail of making a proper diſtinction.

You are well acquainted, that the *envious* and *cenſorious* are ever diſpoſed to form their judgments of mankind according to their conduct in *public* life, ſo when the members of our ſociety *deſert* their body, or diſcover any *inconſiſtency* in their practice with their profeſſion, they contribute to bring an odium on a profeſſion, which it is the duty of every member highly to honour. Indeed inſtances of the conduct here decried, I own are very rare, and I might ſay, as often as they do happen tend ſtill more to diſcover the *malignity* of our *adverſaries* than to reflect on *ourſelves*. For, with what ill-nature are ſuch ſuggeſtions framed? How weak muſt it appear in the eye of diſcernment, to condemn a *whole* ſociety for the irregularity of a *few* individuals*.

But to return to my argument; *one* great cauſe of *abſenting* onrſelves from the *lodge*, I apprehend to be *this*. The want of that grand fundamental principle, *brotherly-love!* Did we properly cultivate this *Chriſtian* virtue, we ſhould

* Though there ſhould be *free-maſons* who cooly and without agitation of mind, *ſeem* to have diveſted themſelves of all affection and eſteem for the *craft*; we only ſee thereby the effects of an exquiſite and inveterate depravation, for the *principle* is almoſt always preſerved, though its effects *ſeem* to be totally loſt.

think

think ourſelves happieſt when aſſembled together. On *unity* in *affection*, *unity* in *government* ſubſiſts; for whatever draws men into *ſocieties*, it is *that* only can cement them.

Let us recollect that *love* is the new and greateſt commandment; all the others are ſummarily comprehended in *this*. It is the fulfilling of the law, and a neceſſary qualification for the *celeſtial lodge*, where the ſupreme architect of the univerſe preſides, who is *love*. *Faith*, *hope*, and *charity* are three principal graces, by which we muſt be guided thither, of which *charity*, or *univerſal-love*, is the chief, when *faith* ſhall be ſwallowed up in viſion, and *hope* in enjoyment, then true *charity*, or *brotherly-love*, will ſhine with the brighteſt luſtre to all *eternity*.

"*Shall ſtand before the hoſt of heaven confeſt*,
"*For ever bleſſing, and for ever bleſt.*"

PRIOR *on* xiii*th*. *ch*. Cor.

On the *other* hand, envy, pride, cenſoriouſneſs, malice, revenge, and diſcord, are the productions of a diabolical diſpoſition. *Theſe* are epidemical diſorders of the mind, and if not ſeaſonably corrected and ſuppreſſed will prove very pernicious to *particular* communities, and more eſpecially to ſuch an eſtabliſhment as *ours*.

Now there is nothing ſo diametrically *oppoſite* to them, and ſo powerful an *antidote* againſt them as *charity*, or true *brotherly-love*; for inſtance,

are

are we tempted to envy, *charity* guards the mind againſt it, *charity* envieth not. Are we tempted by pride? *charity* vaunteth not itſelf, is not puffed up. Where *this* virtue is predominant, *humility* is both its companion and its delight; for, the *charitable* man puts on bowels of mercy, kindneſs, lowlineſs of mind. It is a certain remedy likewiſe againſt all *cenſoriouſneſs:* Charity thinketh no evil, but believeth all things, hopeth all things, will ever incline us to believe and hope the beſt, eſpecially of *a brother.*

Therefore let a conſtant exerciſe of this *Chriſtian* virtue, ſo eſſential to our preſent and future happineſs, prove our great eſteem for it, and by its influence upon our lives and actions teſtify to the world the cultivation of it amongſt us, that they who *think* or *ſpeak* evil of *us*, may be thereby confounded and put to open ſhame. And as it was a proverbial expreſſion among the enemies of *Chriſtianity* in its infancy, "See how theſe *Chriſtians* love one another," may the ſame with equal propriety be ſaid of *free-maſons.* This will convince the ſcoffer and ſlanderer, that we are lovers of *Him*, who ſaid, *If ye love me keep my commandments*; and, *this is my commandment, that ye love one another as I have loved you.* This will prove to our *enemies*, that a good *maſon* is a good man, and a good Chriſtian, and afford ourſelves the greateſt comfort *here* by giving us a well-grounded hope of admittance into a lodge of everlaſting felicity *hereafter*. THUS ſhall our inſtitution be enabled to repel the deſtructive power of *time*, the ſtrongeſt arm of *calumny*, and the ſevereſt ſtrokes of *reproach*, till that great and important day, when the commiſſioned arch-angel ſhall pronounce this *awful* ſentence,

" Earth *be diſſolv'd, with all the worlds on high*,
" *And* time *be loſt in vaſt eternity*."

OGILVIE.

A CHARGE, *delivered to the Members of the* UNION LODGE, *regularly conſtituted and held at the* Union Punch Houſe, Princes Street, Briſtol, *A. L.* 5767,

By Brother *ALEXANDER SHEDDEN*, Right Worſhipful Maſter.

My Worthy BRETHREN,

THIS being our ſecond quarterly meeting, ſince I had the honour to ſit in this chair, I embrace the opportunity again to return you my ſincere thanks for that honour, and to aſſure you I am determined, to the utmoſt of my power, to execute the great truſt which you continue to repoſe in me, with *freedom*, *fervency* and *zeal*. That I may be enabled ſo to do, let us unanimouſly concur in cultivating peace, harmony, and perfect friendſhip, ſtriving who ſhall excel in brotherly-love and benignity; then I doubt not but with the aſſiſtance of my brother officers, I may be enabled to conduct the *buſi-*

neſs of the lodge, and diſcharge *my* duty to *your* ſatisfaction.

To accompliſh theſe deſireable ends, let me in the firſt place intreat your ſtrict attention to our *by-laws*, ever keeping in view the *general* regulations, conſtitutions, and orders of our ancient and honourable ſociety. Let due regard be paid to your officers in their reſpective ſtations, whoſe duty it is to regulate the proceedings of the lodge, and to carry the laws into execution, and may the only contention amongſt us be, a laudable emulation in cultivating the royal art, and endeavouring to excel each other in whatever is good and great. The *moral* and *ſocial* duties of life we ſhould make a *principal* ſubject of contemplation, for thereby we ſhall be enabled to ſubdue our paſſions, and cultivate fraternal affection, the glory and cement of this inſtitution, *laying aſide all malice, and all guile and hypocriſies, and envies, and all evil-ſpeakings*; manifeſting our love one to another, for "Love is of God; and he "that loveth God, loveth his brother alſo. And "he that ſaith he is in the *light*, and hateth his "brother, is in *darkneſs* until now."

Suffer nothing to be heard within the ſacred walls of this lodge, but the heavenly ſounds of *truth*, *peace* and *concord*, with a chearful harmony of ſocial and innocent mirth; and, "be ye "like-minded, having the ſame love, being of "one accord and of one mind; let nothing be

"done

"done through ſtrife or vain-glory, but in low-"lineſs of mind, let each eſteem other better "than themſelves." Never give cauſe for it to be ſaid, that we who are *ſolemnly* connected by the ſtricteſt laws of *amity*, ſhould ever omit the practice of *forbearance*, and allow our paſſions to *controul* us, when one great end propoſed by our meeting here is, to *ſubdue* them. Let us not ſit down contented with the *name* only of *a maſon*, but walk worthy of that glorious profeſſion, in conſtant conformity to its duties. To become brethren worthy of our moſt ancient and honourable inſtitution, we muſt devote ourſelves to the ſtudy and diſcharge of the following duties, which are more or leſs within the reach of every capacity, viz. a knowledge of the myſterious problems, hieroglyphics, and ſymbolical cuſtoms and ceremonies of the royal art, together with the origin, nature, and deſign of the inſtitution, its ſigns, tokens, &c. whereby *maſons* are univerſally known to, and can converſe with each other, though born and bred in different countries and languages.

A *free-maſon* muſt likewiſe be a *good man*, one who duly fears, loves, and ſerves his heavenly maſter, and in imitation of the *operative* maſon, who erects a temporal building according to the rules and deſigns laid down for him, by the maſter maſon, on *his* treſſel-board, raiſes a ſpiritual building, according to the laws and injunctions

laid

laid down by the *ſupreme architect of the univerſe* in the *book of life*, which may juſtly be conſidered in this light, as a *ſpiritual treſſel board.*

He muſt honour the king, and be ſubordinate to his ſuperiors, and ever ready to promote the *deſerving* brother in all his lawful employments and concerns. Theſe, my brethren, are qualifications of a *good maſon*, wherefore they merit our peculiar attention; and, as it is our *duty* we ſhould make it our pleaſure to practice them, by ſo doing we ſhall let our light ſhine before men, and prove ourſelves worthy members of that inſtitution, which ennobles all who conform to its moſt glorious precepts.

Finally, let me adviſe you to be very circumſpect, and well guarded againſt the baſe attempts of *pretenders*, always ſetting a watch before your mouth. And with reſpect to any who may *call* themſelves maſons, but (poſſeſſing refractory ſpirits) are at the ſame time enemies to all order, decency, and decorum, ſpeaking and acting as *rebels* to the *conſtitution* of maſons in this kingdom, let me exhort you to have no connection with them, but according to the advice of St. Paul, to the *Theſſalonians*, "withdraw yourſelves "from every brother that walketh diſorderly," leaving *ſuch* to the natural conſequence of their own bad conduct; being well aſſured, that the vain fabric, which *they* mean to erect, having no other ſupport than their own *ignorance*, *debility*, *ty*, and *deformity*, will of itſelf ſoon tumble to the ground, with ſhame and ruin on the builders heads. On the other hand, let us live in ſtrict amity and fraternal love with all *juſt* and upright brethren, that we may ſay with the *royal Pſalmiſt*, "Behold how good, and how pleaſant it is, for "brethren to dwell together in unity."

Let GOD's holy word be the guide of our faith; and, juſtice, charity, love and mercy, our characteriſticks, then we may reaſonably hope to attain the cœleſtial *paſs-word*, and gain admittance into the lodge of our *ſupreme grand maſter, where pleaſures flow for evermore.* This is the fervent prayer of him who glories in the name of a *faithful-maſon*, and has the honour to be maſter of this right worſhipful lodge.

The

The following ADDRESS *was delivered, by the Rev.* Mr. HENRY CHALMERS, P. M. *in the Lodge of* Perfect Friendship, *constituted and held in the town of* Chelmsford, *in the County of* Essex, *on the Festival of St.* JOHN the Baptist, *A. L.* 5767. *On which occasion a* Sermon *had also been preached in the forenoon by the* Rev. Mr. Panting.

Rt. Worshipful Master, and worthy Brethren,

A Desire to entertain each other with social, virtuous and chearful sentiments, is the duty as well as the happiness of every member of our ancient and honourable society.

Animated by brotherly good-will (which I hope is deeply engraved on the heart of every *free-mason*,) permit me to congratulate you on the *return* of this festival, thus respectfully celebrated by a lodge wherein I have had the honour to preside:—a lodge in its infancy distinguished for its regularity and choice of its members; but

but, under the prudent conduct of our *present* * *guardian*, flourishing beyond expectation, and by his assiduity and care, honoured with the addition of many illustrious and worthy brethren.

Happy am I likewise to see *all* the offices this day supported by brethren, who I am persuaded want neither inclination or abilities, to recommend and enforce whatever may be found necessary to maintain the universal reputation of the institution, and particularly the felicity of this lodge.

Our reverend brother in his ingenious discourse this morning judiciously expatiated on those glorious principles, on which our royal art is *founded*, and proved its *basis* still to be firm and permanent. Let it be our peculiar care, as it is our indispensible duty, not to undermine it by any inattention, omission, or irregularity.

Knowledge (which is attained by diligence) must precede practice, and till we know a duty, it is impossible for us to discharge it. The *lodge* is the properest school wherein we can expect to arrive at any proficiency in our noble science, and by a constant and regular attendance *here*, we may hope to become masters of the royal art;

---

* John Reynolds, Esq; coroner of the county of *Essex*.

whereas the neglect of this *duty* can produce nought but *ignorance* and *error*. Indeed! were *these* the only consequences of a wilful or indolent absence, the craft might not suffer much by such lukewarm brethren; but I am sorry to say this is not all, the eye of the *censurer* is ever upon us, and the lips of the *stammerer* speak *plainly* against us, and when the members of our society desert the body, the unenlightened are ever ready to impeach the harmony and improvement which we profess and know to be the inseparable companions of every well regulated lodge, where *virtue* finds a real pleasure, and *vice* a just abhorrence.

Let us therefore be ever vigilant in the discharge of our duty, and particularly assiduous in cultivating those grand essentials of our constitution, *brotherly-love*, *beneficence*, and *truth*. Thus we shall be always happy in assembling together. Thus will our lodge shine with undiminished lustre, even as long as the radiant sun shall rise in the east to gild our days, and the pale moon appear to illuminate our nights. Thus *supported* by wisdom, strength, and beauty; *adorned* with peace, plenty, and harmony; *cemented* by secrecy, morality, and good-fellowship, what has it to fear? Let the tides of time and chance beat against its walls; the gusts of malice assault its tow'ring height, its all in vain! Still ſhall the noble ſtructure *firmly* ſtand, and only be diſſolved when the pillars of the univerſe ſhall be ſhaken, and, “ the great globe itſelf, yea, all which it inherit, “ ſhall, like the baſeleſs fabric of a viſion, leave “ not a wreck behind.”

The following ADDRESS *was delivered in a* Lodge *of* FREE AND ACCEPTED MASONS, *immediately after the* EXPULSION *of a* Member *who had been repeatedly, but in vain, admoniſhed for the illiberal practice of* backbiting *and* ſlandering *his* BRETHREN.

BRETHREN,

AS in ALL numerous bodies and ſocieties of men, ſome *unworthy* will ever be found, it can be no wonder, that notwithſtanding the excellent principles and valuable precepts, laid down and inculcated by *our* venerable inſtitution, we have *ſuch* amongſt *us:* men! who, inſtead of being ornaments or uſeful members of our body, I am ſorry to ſay, are a *ſhame* and *diſgrace* to it.

Theſe are ſufficiently characterized by a natural propenſity to *backbite* and *ſlander* their brethren, vices! truly deteſtable in all men, and more peculiarly ſo in FREE-MASONS, who by the regulations of their inſtitution, are ſpecially exhorted and enjoined " to ſpeak as well of a brother

ther if *absent* as *present*; to defend his honour and reputation wherever attacked, as far as truth and justice will permit: and where they cannot reasonably vindicate him, at least to refrain from contributing to *condemn* him."

But alas! regardless of their duty in general, and of these laudable injunctions in particular, we frequently find *such* men assiduously employed in *traducing* the characters of their brethren; and instead of rejoicing at their good fortune, pitying their misfortune, and apologizing for their weaknesses and errors, envying their prosperity, and (unaffected by their adversity) with a secret and malicious pleasure exploring and publishing their defects and failings; like *trading vessels* they pass from place to place, receiving and discharging whatever CALUMNY they can *procure* from others, or *invent* themselves.

As we have just now had a mortifying instance of the necessary consequence of such *base* conduct, in the *expulsion* of one of our own members, permit me to deliver to you some sentiments of the great Archbishop TILLOTSON * on the subject. He assigns various *causes* of this evil, and also furnishes directions, which if adhered to, will greatly contribute to prevent and *remedy* it.

---

* Vide his sermon on EVIL-SPEAKING.

"If

" If we consider the *causes* of this evil practise, we shall find one of the most common is *ill-nature*; and by a general mistake, *ill-nature* passeth for *wit*, as *cunning* doth for *wisdom*; though in truth they are as different as *vice* and *virtue*.

" There is no greater evidence of the bad temper of mankind, than their proneness to *evil-speaking*. For as our Saviour saith, *Out of the abundance of the heart the mouth speaketh*, and therefore we commonly incline to the censorious and uncharitable side."

" The *good* spoken of others we easily forget, or seldom mention, but the *evil* lies uppermost in our memories, and is ready to be published upon all occasions; nay, what is more ill-natured and unjust, tho' many times we do not believe it ourselves, we tell it to others, and venture it to be believed according to the charity of those to whom it is told."

" *Another* cause of the frequency of this vice is, *That many are so bad themselves*. For to think and speak ill of others is not only a *bad* thing, but a sign of a *bad* man. When men are *bad* themselves they are glad of any opportunity to censure others, and endeavour to bring things to a level; hoping it will be some justification of their own faults, if they can but make others appear equally guilty."

" A *third* cause of *evil-speaking* is *malice* and *revenge*. When we are blinded by our passions we we do not consider what is *true*, but what is *mischievous*; we care not whether the evil we speak be true or not; nay, many are so base as to *invent* and *raise* false reports, on purpose to blast the reputations of those by whom they think themselves injured. This is a *diabolical* temper; and therefore St. JAMES tells us, that the *slanderer's tongue is set on fire of hell.*"

"A *fourth* cause of this vice is *envy*. Men look with an evil eye upon the *good* that is in others, and do what they can to discredit their *commendable* qualities; thinking their own character lessened by *them*, they greedily entertain, and industriously publish, what may raise themselves upon the *ruins* of other men's reputation."

"A *fifth* cause of evil-speaking is *impertinence* and *curiosity*; an itch of talking of affairs which do not concern us. Some love to mingle themselves in *all* business, and are loth to seem ignorant of such important news as the *faults* and *follies* of men; therefore with great care they pick up ill stories to entertain the next company they meet, not perhaps out of malice, but for want of something better to talk of."

"*Lastly*, many do this out of *wantonness*, and for *diversion*; so little do they consider *a man's reputation* is too great and tender a concern to be jested with; and that a slanderous tongue *bites like a serpent, and cuts like a sword.* What can be ſo barbarous, next to ſporting with a man's life, as to play with his honour and good name, which to ſome is better than life?"

Such, and ſo bad, are the *cauſes* of this *vice*.

"If we conſider its pernicious *effects* we ſhall find, that to ſuch as are ſlandered it is a great injury, commonly a *high provocation*, but always matter of Grief."

"It is certainly a great *injury*, and if the evil which we ſay of them be not true, it is an *injury* beyond reparation. It is an *injury* that deſcends to a man's children; becauſe the good or ill name of the father is derived down to them, and many times the beſt thing he has to leave them is an *unblemiſhed* virtue. And do we make no conſcience to rob his innocent children of the beſt part of this ſmall patrimony, and of all the kindneſs that would have been done them for their father's ſake, if his reputation had not been ſo underſervedly ſtained? Is it no crime by the breath of our mouth at once to blaſt a man's reputation, and to ruin his children perhaps to all poſterity? Can we jeſt with ſo ſerious a matter? an injury ſo very hard to be repented of as it ought; becauſe, in ſuch a caſe, no *repentance* will be acceptable without *reſtitution*, if in our power."

" Even ſuppoſe the matter of the *ſlander* true, yet no man's reputation is conſiderably ſtained, though never ſo deſervedly, without great hurt to him; and it is odds but the charge, by paſſing through ſeveral hands, is aggravated beyond truth, every one being apt to *add* ſomething to it."

" Beſides the *injury*, it is commonly a *high provocation*; the conſequences of which may be dangerous and deſperate quarrels. One way or other the injured perſon will hear of it, and will take the firſt opportunity to revenge it."

" At beſt, it is always matter of *grief* to the perſon that is defamed, and *chriſtianity*, which is the beſt natured inſtitution in the world, forbids us to do thoſe things whereby we may *grieve one another*."

A man's character is a tender thing, and a wound *there* ſinks deep into the ſpirit even of a wiſe and a good man; and the more innocent any man is in this reſpect, the more ſenſible he is of this uncharitable treatment; becauſe he never treats others ſo, nor is he conſcious to himſelf that he hath deſerved it.

" To *ourſelves* the conſequences of this *vice* are as bad or worſe. He that accuſtoms himſelf to ſpeak evil of others, gives a bad character to himſelf, even to thoſe whom he deſires to pleaſe, who, if they be *wiſe*, will conclude that he ſpeaks of them to others, as he does of others to them."

"And this practice of *evil-ſpeaking* may be inconvenient many other ways. For, who knows in the chance of things, and the mutability of human affairs, whoſe kindneſs he may ſtand in need of before he dies? ſo, that did a man only conſult his own ſafety and quiet, he ought to refrain from *evil-ſpeaking*."

"How *cheap* a kindneſs is it to *ſpeak well*, at leaſt not to ſpeak *ill* of others. A good word is an eaſy obligation, but not to ſpeak ill requires only our ſilence. Some inſtances of charity are chargeable; but were a man never ſo covetous he might afford another his good word; at leaſt he might refrain from ſpeaking ill of him, eſpecially if it be conſidered, how dear many have paid for a *ſlanderous* and reproachful word."

"No quality ordinarily recommends one more to the favour of men, than to be free from this *vice*. Such a man's friendſhip every one deſires; and, next to piety and righteouſneſs, nothing is thought a greater commendation, than that he was never or very rarely heard to ſpeak ill of any.

"Let every man lay his hand upon his heart, and conſider how himſelf is apt to be affected with this uſage. Nothing ſure is more equal and reaſonable than that known rule, *What thou*

wouldſt

wouldst have no man do to thee, that do thou to no man."

"The following *directions*, if duly obſerved, will greatly contribute to the *prevention* and *cure* of this great evil."

"Never ſay any *evil* of another, but what you certainly know.

"Whenever you poſitively accuſe a man of any crime, though it be in private and among friends, ſpeak as if you were upon your *oath*, becauſe GOD ſees and hears you. *This*, not only charity but juſtice demands of us. He that eaſily credits a falſe report is almoſt as culpable as the firſt inventor of it. Therefore never ſpeak evil of any upon common fame, which, for the moſt part is falſe, but almoſt always uncertain."

"Before you ſpeak evil of another, conſider whether he hath not *obliged* you by ſome real kindneſs, and then it is a bad turn to ſpeak ill of him who hath done you good. Conſider alſo, whether you may not come hereafter to be acquainted with him, related to him, or in want of *his* favour whom you have thus injured? and whether it may not be in his power to *revenge* a ſpiteful and needleſs word, by a ſhrewd turn? ſo that if a man made no conſcience of hurting others, yet he ſhould in prudence have ſome conſideration of himſelf."

"Let

"Let us accuſtom ourſelves to be truly ſorry for the faults of men, and then we ſhall take no pleaſure in publiſhing them. Common humanity requires this of us, conſidering the great infirmities of our nature, and that we alſo are liable to be tempted; conſidering likewiſe how ſevere a puniſhment every crime is to itſelf, how terribly it expoſeth a man to the wrath of God, both here and hereafter."

"Whenever we hear any man evil ſpoken of, if we have heard any good of him, let us ſay *that*. It is always more *humane* and more *honourable* to vindicate others, than to accuſe them. Were it neceſſary that a man ſhould be evil ſpoken of, his good and bad qualities ſhould be repreſented together, otherwiſe he may be ſtrangely miſrepreſented, and an indifferent man may be made a *monſter*."

"They that will obſerve nothing in a *wiſe* man, but his overſights and follies; nothing in a *good* but his failings and infirmities, may render both deſpicable. Should we heap together all the paſſionate ſpeeches, all the imprudent actions of the beſt man, and preſent them all at one view, concealing his *virtues*, he, in this diſguiſe, would look like a mad-man or fury; and yet if his life were *fairly* repreſented in the manner it was led, he would appear to all the world to be an admirable and excellent perſon. But how numerous ſoever any man's *ill-qualities* are,

it

it is but just that he should have due praise of his few *real virtues.*"

"That you may not *speak* ill, do not delight in *hearing* it of any. Give no countenance to busy-bodies: if you cannot decently reprove them because of their quality, divert the discourse some other way; or by seeming not to mind it, signify that you do not like it."

"Let every man mind his own duty and concern. Do but endeavour in good earnest to mend yourself, and it will be work enough, and leave you little time to talk of others."

In the foregoing Sentiments, the BACKBITER and SLANDERER may see himself fully represented as in a true mirrour; and *detestable* as the spectacle *naturally* appears, much more so does it seem when *masonically* examined. May all *such* therefore contemplate the *nature* and *consequences* of this *abominable* vice, and that they may still become *worthy* men and *masons*, let them constantly pray with the royal *Psalmist*, (Psal. cxli.) *Set a watch, O Lord, before my mouth, keep thou the door of my lips*; being assured of their encouragement, that, *He who backbiteth not with his tongue, nor doeth evil to his neighbour, nor taketh up a reproach against his neighbour, shall abide in the tabernacle of the Lord, and shall dwell in his holy hill.*

A Short CHARGE *generally given to new admitted Brethren.*

YOU are now admitted by the unanimous consent of our *lodge*, a fellow of our most ancient and honourable society; ancient, as having subsisted from time immemorial, and honourable, as tending in every particular to render a man so, that will be but conformable to its glorious precepts. The greatest monarchs in all ages, as well of Asia and Africa as of Europe, have been encouragers of the royal art, and many of them have presided as grand masters over the masons in their respective dominions; not thinking it any diminution of their imperial dignities to level themselves with their brethren in masonry, and to act as they did. The world's great architect is our *supreme master*, and the unerring rule he has given us, is that by which we work. Religious disputes are never suffered in the lodge, for, as *free-masons*, we only pursue the universal religion of nature: This is the cement which unites men of the most different prin-

principles in one ſacred band, and brings together thoſe who were the moſt diſtant from one another.

There are *three* general heads of duty, which maſons ought always to inculcate, *viz.* to *God*, our *neighbours*, and *ourſelves*. To *God*, in never mentioning his name but with that reverential awe which becomes a creature to bear to his creator; and to look upon him always as the *ſummum bonum* which we came into the world to enjoy: And according to that view to regulate all our purſuits. To our *neighbours*, in acting upon the *ſquare*, or doing as we would be done by. To *ourſelves* in avoiding all intemperances and exceſſes, whereby we may be led into a behaviour unbecoming our laudable profeſſion.

In the ſtate, a maſon is to act as a peaceable and dutiful ſubject, conforming chearfully to the government under which he lives: he is to pay a due deference to his ſuperiors, and from his inferiors he is rather to receive honour with ſome reluctance than to extort it; he is to be a man of benevolence and charity, not ſitting down contented while his fellow-creatures (but much more his brethren) are in want, and it is in his power, without prejudicing himſelf or family, to relieve them. In the *lodge* he is to behave with all due decorum, leſt the beauty and harmony thereof ſhould be diſturbed and broke. He is to be obedient to the maſter and preſiding

of-

officers, and to apply himſelf cloſely to the buſineſs of *maſonry*, that he may ſooner become a proficient therein, both for his own credit, and for that of the lodge. He is not to neglect his neceſſary avocations for the ſake of maſonry, nor to involve himſelf in quarrels with thoſe who through ignorance may ſpeak evil of, or ridicule it. He is to be a lover of the arts and ſciences and to take all opportunities of improving himſelf therein. If he recommends a friend to be made a maſon, he muſt vouch him to be ſuch as he really believes will conform to the aforeſaid duties: leſt by his miſconduct at any time the lodge ſhould paſs under ſome evil imputations. Nothing can prove more ſhocking to all faithful maſons, than to ſee any of their brethren profane, or break through the ſacred rules of their order, and ſuch as can do it they wiſh had *never* been admitted.

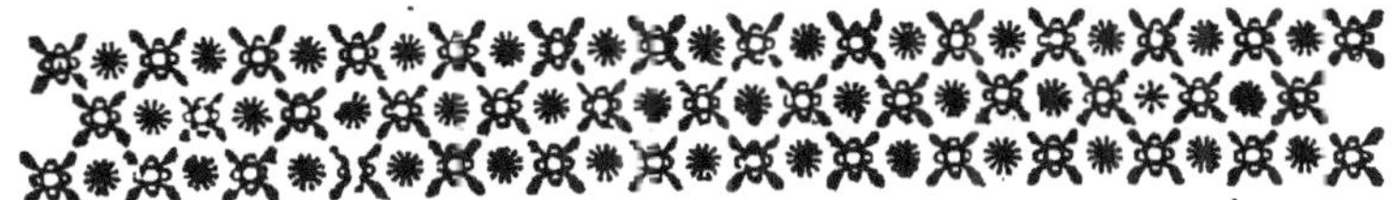

A CHARGE *delivered by Brother* THOMAS FRENCH, G.S. *at the initiation of a* Free-Mason.

BROTHER,

BEING now regularly initiated into this society, permit me to offer to your serious consideration, those *virtues* that will always distinguish you among men, especially masons.

The *Holy Scriptures*, the standard of truth, and the unerring dictates of an unerring Being, I would recommend as the primary object of your attention.

Next, a general, an unlimited regard for men of *virtue*, *honour* and *integrity*, howsoever distinguished by private persuasion; *masonry* wisely removes such distinctions, and by uniting all countries, sects and principles into one inseparable band of affection, conciliates true friendship, and effectuates the noble purpose of making each other happy, and rejoicing in each other's felicity.

Hence *disputes* on religion and politics are never suffered to interrupt the friendly intercourse of *our* regular *assemblies*—These are designed to improve the mind, correct the morals and reform the judgment.

Your experience in life, has no doubt made familiar to you the *three* great duties of morality; to God; your neighbour; and yourself; which I hope your *new* character as a *free-mason*, will still more deeply imprint upon your *mind*, and render your *conduct* not only regular and uniform, but in every other respect agreeable to the dignity of this laudable profession.

As a *mason* you are chearfully to conform to the government under which you live; to consider the interest of the community as your own; and be ready on all occasions to give proofs of *loyalty* to your sovereign, and affection to your country.

Benevolence and *charity*, being the renowned characteristics of *masonry*, you are to cherish and promote; and though you ought ever liberally to contribute to alleviate the miseries of the wretched, yet you are more particularly to extend your pity to a poor *brother*, whose unhappy circumstances may oblige him to solicit your friendly assistance; ever remembering that period of your life, when you was *introduced* into masonry, ***** on *which*, if you but for a moment reflect, it cannot fail making you so far *bene-*

volent

volent as never to ſhut your ear unkindly to the complaints of the wretched. But when a poor *brother* is oppreſſed by *want*, you will in a particular manner liſten to *his* ſufferings with attention, in conſequence of which, pity will flow from your breaſt, and Relief according to your capacity.

The ſolemnity of our ceremonies, will ever require from you a *ſerious* deportment, and ſtrict attention to the elucidating of thoſe emblems and hieroglyphics under which our myſteries are couched.

And as *order* and *regularity* cannot fail to render permanent the harmony of this lodge, it is expected you will be obedient to the maſter and preſiding officers, and be particularly careful never to introduce any *diſcourſe* that may tend to violate your character as a *gentleman*, or a *maſon*, or to depreciate thoſe virtues that always adorn an honeſt mind.

If therefore from among your friends or acquaintance, you ſhould hereafter propoſe a candidate for our myſteries, I would earneſtly recommend, that you know him to be worthy; and never from a *pecuniary* or *ungenerous* motive, endeavour to introduce any but men of *honour* and *integrity*, whoſe *character* as well as principle, juſtly entitles him to the privileges of this fraternity.

To expatiate on the neceſſity of a cloſe application to the duties of maſonry, will, I preſume, be needleſs, as I doubt not but your own experience will ſoon evince the real value and utility of this *ſcience*, and the excellency of its precepts.

I ſhall therefore conclude this *addreſs* in a ſure expectation of your implicit obedience to the foregoing circumſtances, as well for your own honour as the credit of *this* lodge, and that you will chearfully conform to all thoſe ſalutary *laws* which are, and ever have been, the eſtabliſhed *baſis* and *ſupport* of the ROYAL ART.

A PRAYER *at the empointing of a brother, used in the reign of Edward IV.*

THE mighty GOD and father of heaven, with the wisdom of his glorious son, through the goodness of the Holy Ghost, that hath been three persons in one godhead, be with us at our beginning, give us grace to govern in our living here, that we may come to his bliss that shall never have an end.

A PRAYER *to be used at the admission of a brother.*

O Most glorious and eternal God, who art the chief architect of the created universe! grant unto us, thy servants, who have already entered ourselves into this most noble, ancient and honourable fraternity, that we may be solid and

and thoughtful, and always have a rememberance of thoſe ſacred and holy things we have taken on us, and endeavour to inſtruct and inform each other in ſecrecy, that nothing may be unlawfully or illegally obtained; and that this perſon who is now to be made a maſon, may be a worthy member, and may he, and all of us, live as men, conſidering the great end for which thy goodneſs has created us; and do thou, O God, give us wiſdom to contrive in all our doings, ſtrength to ſupport in all difficulties, and beauty to adorn thoſe heavenly manſions where thy honour dwells; and grant, O Lord, that we may agree together in brotherly-love and charity one towards another; and in all our dealings in the world, do juſtice to all men, love mercy, and walk humbly with thee, our God; and, at laſt, may an abundant enterance be adminiſtered unto us, into thy kingdom, O great Jehovah. *Now unto the king eternal, immortal, inviſible, the only wiſe God, be kingdom, power, and glory, for ever and ever.* Amen.

Another PRAYER.

MOST holy and glorious Lord God, thou architect of heaven and earth, who art the giver of all good graces: and hath promiſed that

that where two or three are gathered together in thy name, thou wilt be in the midſt of them: in thy name we aſſemble and meet together, moſt humbly beſeeching thee to bleſs us in all our undertakings, to give us thy holy ſpirit, to enlighten our minds with wiſdom and underſtanding, that we may know and ſerve thee aright, that all our doings may tend to thy glory, and to the ſalvation of our ſouls: And we beſeech thee, O Lord God, to bleſs this our preſent undertaking, and to grant that this our brother may dedicate his life to thy ſervice, and be a true and faithful brother among us: endue him with divine wiſdom, that he may, with the ſecrets of maſonry, be able to unfold the myſteries of godlineſs and chriſtianity.

This we humbly beg in the name, and for the ſake of Jeſus Chriſt, our Lord and Saviour. Amen.

POST-

POSTSCRIPT.

AS Laws, Orders and Constitutions are *essentially* necessary to the establishment and support of *every* society, without which no *society* can long subsist with any degree of happiness or reputation, the GENERAL laws and regulations of the *most ancient and honourable society of free and accepted masons*, as set forth in the book of constitutions, are invariably to be observed by every *private* lodge, and *every* individual member of the fraternity. But for the better answering the purposes of particular lodges; to cement the union thereof; and to further the good intentions of those brethren, who are disposed to cultivate the ROYAL CRAFT, according to the ancient ſplendour; the *grand maſter* of *maſons*, hath permitted, and it hath ever been the *uſage* of the lodges to frame to themſelves ſuch *bye-laws*, as to the members of each particular lodge ſhall ſeem meet, *provided* that the *ancient land marks* are preſerved inviolate, and that ſuch *bye-laws* be agreeable to the *general regulations*.

And as it frequently happens that *new* lodges are at a loſs for ſome aſſiſtance on theſe occaſions, the following form is offered for that purpoſe.

BYE-LAWS, for the regulation of the Lodge No. known by the name of of the *moſt ancient and honourable Society of Free and Accepted Maſons*, duly conſtituted the day of A. L. 5769. A. D. 1769, firſt held at

and now held at

Article 1. *Fixed, or lodge nights.*

That the lodge ſhall aſſemble on the third *Friday* in every month at ſeven o'clock in the evening; which ſhall be deemed general, or public lodge nights: but that the right worſhipful maſter ſhall have power, as in times paſt, to convene a *private* lodge as often as he ſhall find it expedient.

Article

Article 2. *Election and choice of officers.*

That the election of a *master*, as well as a *treasurer* of this lodge, ſhall be half yearly, to wit, at the public lodges held in *June* and *December*, by a majority of the members preſent, by ballot. That the maſter elect, if preſent, ſhall on that night of Election, if not, at the next lodge night, appoint the two *wardens* and *ſecretary*. That the accounts of the treaſurer ſhall be audited on the night of election, or ſo ſoon after as conveniently can, by the maſter and wardens for the time being, or by a committee for that purpoſe to be appointed; and the ballance appearing to be due thereon, ſhall be paid by him to the *treaſurer elect*, immediately after the accounts are ſo audited, or at the next public lodge night. That the *tyler* ſhall be elected by ballot, or holding up of hands of the members preſent, on every election night, or as often as there ſhall be occaſion, and ſhall be continued only, during his good behaviour and the pleaſure of the lodge.

Article 3. *Payment of Quarteridge.*

That every member of this lodge ſhall pay to the treaſurer for the uſe of the lodge the annual ſubſcription of eighteen ſhillings, by quarterly payments, viz. the ſum of four ſhillings and ſixpence on the 1ſt lodge night after *Chriſtmas*, the 1st. lodge night after *Lady-day*, the 1st. lodge night after *Midſummer*, and on the 1st. lodge night after *Michaelmas*. And if any member ſhall neglect or refuſe to pay the ſame within three months from every ſuch quarter day, having had notice thereof from the ſecretary, he ſhall be expelled as a member and excluded from viſiting this lodge, unleſs good cauſe be ſhewn to the maſter and brethren to induce a forbearance.

Article 4. *Makings*.

That every perſon deſirous of being made a maſon in this lodge, ſhall be recommended and duly propoſed by a *member* in an open public lodge; when the brother ſo propoſing him, ſhall depoſit *half a guinea* on account of his fees. And the brother ſo propoſed ſhall be balloted for the *next* ſucceeding public lodge night, in which interval proper enquiry may be made into his character, and if on ſuch ballot there ſhall not appear *two* * black, or negative balls, he ſhall be initiated and admitted a member on paying to the treaſurer the admiſſion fee *one guinea and a half*, together with his ſubſcription in proportion to the time then to come in the current quarter; and alſo five ſhillings to the

* In ſome lodges *three*, but in general *one* negative excludes.

the uſe of the grand or public fund of maſons for his *admiſſion* and *regiſtring* fees: and if on a ballot he ſhould appear *not* to be admitted, the ſum depoſited when he was propoſed ſhall be returned to the brother who propoſed him. And if he is approved on the ballot, and neglects to attend for admiſſion, *three* lodge nights, his depoſit ſhall in that caſe be forfeited to the lodge. And if any brother ſhall be duly propoſed and admitted, who hath before been initiated into the firſt or paſſed to the ſecond degree, in another regular lodge, he ſhall pay ſo much as together with what he hath already advanced for ſuch initiation, or paſs, as will amount to the ſum of one guinea and a half, provided that no ſuch brother ſhall be paſſed or raiſed for leſs than half a guinea for each degree beſides his fee for regiſtering.

Article 5. *Admiſſion of members.*

That no brother ſhall be admitted a member of this lodge until he hath viſited us once at leaſt, and has been duly propoſed by a member in *open* lodge, which done he ſhall be ballotted for at the next ſucceeding publick lodge; and unleſs *three* negatives or black balls appear, ſhall be admitted on paying five ſhillings to the fund of the lodge and two ſhillings and ſixpence to the grand fund for regiſtering his name, over and above his proportionable ſubſcription.

Article

Article 6. *Viſitors.*

That every viſiting brother being a member of a regular lodge, ſhall pay on every viſit 1*s.* 6*d.* but if only of the lodge of St. *John* ſhall pay 2*s.*

Article 7. *Maſter and Wardens to attend quarterly communications and committees of charity.*

That the maſter and wardens, or their repreſentatives ſhall attend every committee of charity and quarterly communication at the expence of the lodge, and ſhall give to the fund of charity ſuch ſum, and ſo often, as the lodge ſhall agree to at the public lodge next preceding every quarterly committee.

Article 8. *Fund and property of the lodge veſted in maſter and wardens in truſt for the lodge.*

That the caſh or fund as well as the jewels, furniture, and other things belonging to this lodge or ſociety, ſhall be, and hereby is, veſted in and deemed, the property of the maſter, *and wardens* for the time being, ſo that any action or ſuit that ſhall happen to be neceſſary for the preſervation or recovery of the ſame, or any part thereof, or of any of the arrears of quarteridge, may and ſhall be brought or commenced and proſecuted in *their* names, in truſt for the uſe

and

and benefit of the lodge, and to be paid, applied and difpofed of as the majority of the members fhall in due form, from time to time, think proper to direct.

Article 9. *Enacting, abrogating or altering laws.*

That when a motion fhall be made for any new law, or the abrogating or altering of any old one, it fhall firft be handed up in writing to the mafter, in order to be read and confidered by him and the members prefent; and no new law, abrogation, or alteration of any old one, fhall be valid unlefs the fame be entered in the minutes, by the confent of the majority of members prefent at one public lodge, and duly confirmed at the next.

Article 10. *Every member to fign and obey thefe and the conftitutional laws.*

That every member of this lodge fhall fign thefe laws, and fhall obferve and keep the fame, and all fuch as fhall hereafter be enacted agreeable to the 8th article, as well as all the laws, orders and regulations laid down and prefcribed in and by the laft edition of the book of conftitutions of mafonry, and fuch as fhall hereafter be made and publifhed by the authority of the grand lodge.

The

The above laws ſettled and approved of at a public lodge held the day of are now duly enacted and confirmed at another public lodge, held this Day of A. L. 5769. A. D. 1769. Witneſs the hands of us the following officers and brethren.

The

From the following, general *collection, Lodges may furnish themselves with suitable laws, according to their various circumstances.*

Law. 1. *Time of meeting.*

THAT the members of this lodge shall meet every and in each month at the hour of six from *Michaelmas* to *Lady-day*, and at the hour of seven from *Lady-day* to *Michaelmas.* And that every member shall come into the lodge decently cloathed in such attire as is suitable to his rank, quality, and condition in life; always remembring that he can never associate himself with better company than *brothers* and *fellows.*

2. *Opening the lodge.*

When a sufficient number of members shall be assembled, the master, or in his absence, a proper person shall immediately open the lodge and proceed to business. And if the master, either of

 the

the wardens, or other officer of the lodge, who in virtue of his office, is intituled to keep a key or keys, ſhould not attend the lodge in proper time, and neglect to ſend the ſame, whereby the buſineſs of the lodge ſhall be retarded, ſuch brother ſhall forfeit the ſum of

3. *Cloſing the lodge.*

As nothing has a greater tendency to bring the craft into diſrepute than keeping late hours on lodge nights; The maſter ſhall be acquainted by the S. W. when it is o'Clock, and ſhall immediately proceed to cloſe the lodge; either of them failing herein ſhall forfeit the ſum of and any member who is in the lodge (and not being a traveller or lodger in the houſe) remaining in the ſame houſe after o'clock, ſhall alſo forfeit the ſum of It is hoped and expected that no member will offend againſt *this* law, calculated to ſecure the honour and harmony of the lodge, to prevent uneaſineſs to our relatives at home, and to preſerve the œconomy of our families.

4. *Liquors and ſupper.*

All liquors drank at ſupper on lodge nights, ſhall be charged to the *lodge*, but liquors called for before lodge hours, unleſs on account of makings, &c. ſhall not be charged to the *lodge*.

No

No perſon ſhall be permitted to ſup in the lodge room during lodge hours.

5. *Admiſſion of maſons or members.*

That no perſon be ſuffered or admitted to be made a free and accepted maſon in this lodge, or if a maſon, to be a member thereof, unleſs well known to one or more members, to be a man of virtuous principles and integrity, and not a bondſman; and ſuch as by their own conſent, are deſirous to become brethren; it being contrary to our eſtabliſhed conſtitution, to perſuade or engage thereto, and it is hereby recommended to every good maſon, and particularly to the brethren of this lodge, that they be careful whom they recommend as candidates for maſonry, that they may not bring ſcandal, or diſreputation on the craft.

6. *Making, paſſing and raiſing.*

No perſon ſhall be made a maſon in this lodge without firſt paying into the hands of the treaſurer, two guineas; for which, if he *proves* a *worthy* member of our ſociety, He ſhall be intituled to the *three* degrees without further expence: *But* if any one made a maſon in this lodge, ſhall *afterwards* prove an *unworthy* member of the craft, by treating it diſreſpectfully either by words or actions; leading an immoral and

 ſcandalous

ſcandalous life, ſuch perſon ſhall not be intitled to any further degree in this lodge.

And whereas the craft hath ſuffered greatly in its reputation and happineſs by the admiſſion of low and inferior perſons, no ways fit to become members of our ancient and honourable inſtitution, whereby men of rank, quality, knowledge and education, are oft deterred from aſſociating with their brethren at their public meetings: It is hoped every brother who is deſired to propoſe any perſon, will be particularly careful, that he is one in all reſpects ſuitable to the venerable ſociety he is to become a member of; one whoſe temper and diſpoſition may *cement* the *harmony* of the lodge, and whoſe conduct and circumſtances in life, are ſuch as may not tend to diminiſh the credit of it. When a perſon is propoſed, it ſhall be mentioned at the bottom of the next ſummons (which ſhall iſſue at leaſt three days before the lodge night,) that each member may be prepared to approve or reject ſuch candidate; alſo the ſame practice, and for the ſame reaſon, ſhall be obſerved with regard to paſſing or raiſing a brother.

7. *Who proper to be admitted an honorary member, and when diſcontinued.*

That no one member of this lodge be admitted an honorary member, unleſs his avocations frequently

quently call him out of town; or his place of abode be at too great a diſtance to attend conſtantly: In either of the above caſes it may be diſpenſed with by a majority of members preſent; but ſuch an honorary member cannot be choſe into any office, ſpeak, vote, or otherwiſe concern himſelf with the buſineſs of the lodge. Such brother ſhall be admitted each night on the ſame terms as the members, and may have the privilege of becoming a member without any further fine, on his being firſt propoſed and balloted for, and   negatives not appearing againſt him upon caſting up the ſame. If a brother ſhall diſcontinue himſelf a member; from the time the meſſage, letter or motion is ſent or made, he ſhall not vote, or otherwiſe concern himſelf with the buſineſs of the lodge; but if there ſhould happen to be any more lodge nights in the quarter after ſuch motion, he ſhall have a right to be admitted to the end of the quarter he has paid up to.

8. *Time for re-admiſſion of a member.*

That any member having diſcontinued himſelf from this lodge and paid his arrears, may, on application and paying five ſhillings, be re-admitted, (provided   negatives do not appear againſt him) and any ſea-faring member, or one whoſe buſineſs obliges him to leave town, ſhall be excuſed paying his quarteridge

from

from the time of his departure till his arrival in *London*, first having signified the same to the lodge, and paid up his arrears.

9. *Election of officers.*

New officers shall be elected on the Lodge-Nights before the Festivals of St. *John* the Baptist and St. *John* the Evangelist, each member having notice for that purpose in his lodge-letter. In the choice of a master, his abilities must be preferred to his seniority. The master, treasurer and secretary, shall be elected by ballot, but no brother shall be elected master who has not served the office of warden, or master, at least one half year, in some regular lodge; and no officer shall be elected to serve a second time against his inclination. The new master shall be invested by the old master in due form, who shall be allowed a charge before he quits the chair. The new master shall then appoint a senior warden*; but, that the master may not have too much authority in this respect, the senior warden shall appoint a junior warden, and they shall be both invested by the master, as well as the treasurer and secretary, in due form. The old treasurer and secretary are then to lay a state of their accounts before the lodge, which, if approved of by the majority,

* This is *rarely* the practice, most masters appointing *both* wardens; and also the secretary.

shall

ſhall be deemed a regular paſſing of their accounts. The maſter ſhall be allowed two ſhillings and ſixpence when he attends the committee of charity for this lodge, and five ſhillings when he attends with the wardens at a quarterly communication.

10. *Stewards appointed and their duty.*

That the maſter do on the night of his election, appoint two diſcreet brethren, to act as ſtewards of the lodge, who ſhall attend conſtantly, except when hindered by illneſs or urgent buſineſs; in which caſe, the maſter ſhall appoint whom he thinks proper to ſupply their place, *pro tempore*; they ſhall continue in their office till the next election night. Their buſineſs ſhall be to ſee that the viſitors are properly accommodated; that the tables be properly ſupplied, and to keep an account of the ſame, which they ſhall compare with the houſe bill at the cloſing of the lodge. If any brother ſhall order in any wine, &c. after the ſtewards have cloſed their accounts, what is ſo ordered, ſhall be at the ſaid brother's own coſt and charge.

11. *Laws when to be read.*

That upon every election night the maſter ſhall cauſe theſe laws to be read to the lodge, immediately before they proceed to the ballot for a new maſter.

12. *Balloting.*

No member ſhall be permitted to ballot in any matter relating to this lodge until he has paid his full quarteridge up to the next quarter-day in which ſuch ballot is to be made; and, in all ballots, the maſter of the *lodge* ſhall be entitled to a caſting vote upon an equality of numbers.

13. *Not to diſcover a perſon rejected.*

That when any brother is propoſed to become a member, or any perſon to be made a maſon, if it appear upon caſting up the ballot, that they are rejected, no member, or viſiting brother ſhall diſcover, by any means whatſoever, who thoſe members were that oppoſed his election, under the penalty of ſuch brother's being for ever expelled the lodge, (if a member,) and, if a viſiting brother, of his being never more admitted as a viſitor, or becoming a member; and immediately after a negative paſſes on any perſons being propoſed, the maſter ſhall cauſe this law to be read, that no brother preſent may plead ignorance.

14. *Debates, complaints, queſtions, &c. to be addreſſed to the chair.*

That in all debates concerning the affairs of this lodge, complaints made, or queſtions that may

may arise, every brother shall stand up while he speaks, and address himself to the master in the chair; if more than one brother shall stand up at one time to speak, the master shall order the *first* who stood up to proceed, and the rest shall immediately sit down and be silent, till such brother has done speaking; and that no member be allowed to speak twice on one subject, unless to explain himself, and the master shall think it expedient.

15. *Penalty for speaking disrespectfully of the lodge, &c.*

That any brother who is known to have spoken disrespectfully of the society in general, or this lodge in particular, shall not be admitted a member, or as a visitor, until he has made such concession as may be thought satisfactory.

16. *Penalty for breaking the laws.*

That if a brother break any of these rules and orders, the master, with the majority of the brethren (if they think fit) shall lay a fine, not exceeding five shillings on the brother so offending: which fine, as well as all others, shall go to the fund of the lodge; and the brother refusing to pay such fine, shall for ever be excluded this lodge.

17. *Landlord detaining letters.*

That the landlord of the houſe (where this lodge is held) ſhall immediately, upon the receipt of any letter or meſſage left with him for the right worſhipful maſter, forward it to him; and upon his neglect or refuſal, ſhall forfeit to this lodge the ſum of five ſhillings.

18. *Landlords.*

Great inconveniences having ariſen to lodges, by landlords being the proprietors of the furniture, &c. no landlord, or maſter of the houſe where this lodge ſhall be held, ſhall be permitted to have any other ſhare in the furniture, &c. of the lodge than as an individual member; according to the direction of the grand lodge.

19. *Diſguiſed in liquor, ſwearing, &c. the penalties.*

That no brother do preſume to ſwear, come into the lodge intoxicated, or on any account call for wine or other liquors, but addreſs himſelf to the ſtewards or wardens, who, if they think it neceſſary, will give their orders accordingly. That all brethren do behave themſelves with decency to each other, and, with reſpect to the maſter in the chair and preſiding officers; and in caſe of default in either of theſe particulars, the brother ſo offending ſhall forfeit the ſum of two ſhillings and ſixpence to the fund of the lodge.

20.

20. *Presents.*

That all presents made to this lodge be entered in the lodge book, with the brother's name from whom such benevolence flowed, in token of his esteem for masonry in general, and this lodge in particular; and also that the master, for the time being, or his secretary, shall take care to enter the same accordingly.

SOLOMON's TEMPLE:

AN

ORATORIO.

As it was performed at the Philharmonic Room, in *Dublin*, for the benefit of ſick and diſtreſſed FREE-MASONS.

The Words by Mr. JAMES EYRE WEEKS.

The Muſic composed by Mr. RICHARD BROADWAY, Organiſt of *St. Patrick*'s Cathedral.

SOLOMON, the Grand Maſter.
HIGH PRIEST.
HIRAM, the Workman.
URIEL, Angel of the Sun.
SHEBA, Queen of the South.
CHORUS of Prieſts and Nobles.

SOLOMON.

RECITATIVE.

CONVEN'D we're met—chief oracle of heav'n,
To whom the ſacred myſteries are giv'n,
We're met to bid a ſplendid fabrick riſe,
Worthy the mighty ruler of the ſkies.

HIGH

HIGH PRIEST.

And lo! where Uriel, angel of the Sun.
Arrives to ſee the mighty buſineſs done.

AIR.

Behold he comes upon the wings of light,
And with his ſunny veſtment chears the ſight.

URIEL.

RECITATIVE.

The Lord ſupreme, grand maſter of the ſkies!
Who bid Creation from a chaos riſe,
The rules of architecture firſt engrav'd
On Adam's Heart.

CHORUS of the Prieſts and Nobles.

To heavens high Architect all praiſe,
All gratitude be giv'n,
Who deign'd the human ſoul to raiſe,
By Secrets ſprung from heav'n.

SOLOMON.

RECITATIVE.

Adam, well vers'd in arts,
Gave to his ſons the Plumb and Line;
By Maſonry, ſage Tubal Cain
To the deep Organ tun'd the Strain.

AIR.

And while he ſwell'd the melting Note,
On high the ſilver concords float.

HIGH

HIGH PRIEST.

RECITATIVE, accompany'd.

Upon the ſurface of the Waves,
(When God a mighty deluge pours)
Noah a choſen remnant ſaves,
And laid the ark's ſtupendous Floors.

URIEL.

AIR.

Hark from on high the maſon Word
" David my ſervant, ſhall not build :
" A lodge for heaven's all Sov'reign Lord;
" Since blood and War have ſtain'd his ſhield
" That for the Deputy, his Son,
" We have reſerv'd—Prince Solomon. *Da Capo.*

CHORUS for Prieſts and Nobles.

Sound great JEHOVAH's praiſe!
Who bid young Solomon the temple raiſe.

SOLOMON.

RECITATIVE.

So grand a Structure ſhall we raiſe,
That men ſhall wonder! Angels gaze!
By art Divine it ſhall be rear'd,
Nor ſhall the hammer's noiſe be heard.

CHORUS.

Sound great JEHOVAH's praiſe!
Who bid king SOLOMON the temple raiſe.

URIEL.

RECITATIVE.

To plan the mighty dome,
HIRAM, the mafter-mafon's come.

URIEL.

AIR.

We know thee, by thy apron white,
An architect to be.
We know thee, by thy trowel bright,
Well fkill'd in mafonry.
We know thee, by thy jewel's blaze,
Thy manly walk and air.
Inftructed, thou the lodge fhalt raife;
Let all for work prepare.

HIRAM.

AIR.

Not like Babel's haughty building,
Shall our greater lodge be fram'd;
That to hideous jargon yielding,
Juftly was a Babel nam'd;
There Confufion, all o'er-bearing,
Neither fign, nor word they knew,
We, our work with order fquaring,
Each Proportion fhall be true.

SOLOMON.

RECITATIVE.

Cedars, which fince creation grew,
Fall of themfelves to grace the dome;
All Lebanon, as if fhe knew
The great Occafion—lo, is come!

URIEL.

Behold, my brethren of the ſky,
The Work begins, worthy an angel's Eye.

CHORUS of Prieſts and Nobles.

Be preſent all ye heavenly hoſt,
The work begins—The LORD defrays the Coſt!

ACT II.

MESSENGER.

RECITATIVE.

BEHOLD, attended by a num'rous train,
Queen of the ſouth, fair *Sheba*, greets thy reign!
In admiration of thy wiſdom, ſhe,
Comes to preſent the bended knee.

SOLOMON to HIRAM,

RECITATIVE.

Receive her with a fair ſalute;
Such as with majeſty may ſuit.

HIRAM.

AIR.

When allegiance bids obey,
We with pleaſure own its ſway.

Enter SHEBA *attended.*

Obedient to ſuperior greatneſs, ſee,
Our ſcepter hails thy mightier Majeſty.

Thus

Thus PHEBE, Queen of ſhade and night,
Owning the ſun's ſuperior rays,
With feebler glory, leſſer light
Attends the triumph of his blaze.
Oh, all-excelling prince, receive
The tribute due to ſuch a king!
Not the gift, but will, believe!
Take the heart, not what we bring. *D. C.*

SOLOMON.

RECITATIVE.

Let meaſures ſoftly ſweet
Illuſtrious SHEBA's preſence greet.

SOLOMON.

AIR.

Tune to the lute and ſtring the lyre,
Equal to the fair we ſing!
Who can ſee and not admire
SHEBA, conſort for a king!
Enlivening wit and beauty join,
Melting ſenſe and graceful air,
Here united powers combine
To make her brighteſt of the fair. *D. C.*

SOLOMON.

RECITATIVE.

Hiram, our brother and our friend,
Do thou the queen with me attend.

SCENE II. *A view of the temple.*

HIGH PRIEST.

RECITATIVE.

Sacred to heaven behold the dome appears;
Lo, what auguſt ſolemnity it wears;
Angels themſelves have deign'd to deck the frame,
And beautĕous SHEBA ſhall report its fame.

AIR.

When the queen of the ſouth ſhall return
  To the climes which acknowledge her ſway,
Where the ſun's warmer beams fiercely burn,
  The princeſs with tranſport ſhall ſay,
Well worthy my journey, I've ſeen
  A monarch both graceful and wiſe,
Deſerving the love of a queen;
  And a Temple well worthy the ſkies. *D. C.*

CHORUS.

Open ye gates, receive a queen who ſhares
With equal ſenſe your happineſs and cares.

HIRAM.

RECITATIVE.

Of riches much, but more of wiſdom, ſee,
Proportion'd workmanſhip and maſonry.

HIRAM.

AIR.

Oh charming SHEBA, there behold,
What maſſy ſtores of burniſh'd gold,
  Yet richer is our art;

Not

Not all the orient gems, that ſhine,
Nor treaſures of rich Ophir's mine,
Excel the maſon's heart;
True to the fair, he honours more,
Than glitt'ring gems or brighteſt ore,
The plighted pledge of love;
To ev'ry tie of honour bound,
In love and friendſhip conſtant found,
And favour'd from above.

SOLOMON and SHEBA.

DUET.

SHEBA.	One gem beyond the reſt I ſee, And charming SOLOMON is he.
SOLOMON.	One gem beyond the reſt I ſee, Faireſt of fair-ones, thou art ſhe.
SHEBA.	Oh thou ſurpaſſing all men wiſe;
SOLOMON.	And thine excelling womens eyes.

HIRAM.

RECITATIVE.

Wiſdom and beauty both combine
Our art to raiſe, our hearts to join.

CHORUS.

Give to MASONRY the prize,
Where the faireſt chuſe the wiſe:
Beauty ſtill ſhould wiſdom love;
Beauty and order reign above.

Some of the uſual FREE-MASONS SONGS.

The Maſters *Song, by Dr.* ANDERSON.

In the firſt Book it is in 5 Parts, comprehending the Hiſtory *of* Maſonry; *but being too long, the 3d Part is only printed here.*

1.

WE ſing of MASONS ancient fame!
  Lo, *eighty thouſand* craftſmen riſe
Under the MASTERS of great Name,
  More than *three thouſand* juſt and wiſe.
Employ'd by SOLOMON the SIRE,
  And gen'ral MASTER *maſon* too,
As HIRAM was in ſtately *Tyre*,
  Like *Salem* built by *maſons* true.

2.

The *royal* art was then *divine*,
  The *craftſmen* counſell'd from above,
The *temple* was the GRAND DESIGN,
  The wond'ring world did all approve.
Ingenious men from every place
  Came to ſurvey the glorious *pile*;
And when return'd, began to trace
  And imitate its *lofty ſtile*.

At

3.

At length the *Grecians* came to know,
  Geometry, and learn'd the *art*
PYTHAGORAS was rais'd to ſhôw,
  And glorious EUCLID to impart:
Great ARCHIMEDES too appear'd,
  And *Carthaginian* maſters bright;
Till *Roman* citizens uprear'd
  The *art*, with wiſdom and delight.

4.

But when proud *Aſia* they had quell'd,
  And *Greece* and *Egypt* overcome,
In architecture they excell'd,
  And brought the learning all to *Rome*:
Where wiſe VITRUVIUS *Warden* prime,
  Of architects the *art* improv'd
In great AUGUSTUS' peaceful time,
  When *arts* and *artiſts* were belov'd.

5.

They brought the knowledge from the *eaſt*,
  And as they made the nations yield,
They ſpread it thro' the *north* and *weſt*,
  And taught the world the art to build.
Witneſs their *citadels* and *tow'rs*,
  To fortify their legions fine,
Their *temples*, *palaces* and *bow'rs*
  That ſpoke the maſons GRAND DESIGN.

Thus

6.

Thus mighty *eastern* kings and some
Of ABRAM's race, and monarchs good
Of *Egypt*, *Syria*, *Greece*, and *Rome*,
True ARCHITECTURE understood.
No wonder then if *masons* join
To celebrate those MASON-KINGS,
With solemn note and flowing wine,
Whilst every brother jointly sings.

CHORUS.

Who can unfold the *royal art*,
Or shew its *secrets* in a song?
They're safely kept in *mason*'s heart,
And to the ancient *lodge belong!*

To the KING and the CRAFT.

II. *The* Warden's *Song, by the same* Author.

In the first Book it was of 13 *verses, too long: But the last* verse *and* chorus *is thought enough to be sung.*

FROM henceforth ever sing,
The *craftsman* and the *king*,
With poetry and musick sweet
Resound their harmony compleat,

And

And with *geometry* in skilful Hand
Due homage pay,
Without delay,
To noble BEAUFORT now our *master grand.*
He rules the freeborn *sons* of *art*
By love and friendship, hand and heart.

CHORUS of the *Wardens* Song.

Who can rehearse the praise
In soft poetick lays,
Or solid prose, of *masons* true,
Whose art transcends the common view?
Their *secrets* ne'er to strangers yet expos'd,
Preserv'd shall be
By *masons free,*
And only to the *ancient lodge* disclos'd;
Because they're kept in *masons heart*
By brethren of the *royal art.*

To the *grand master.*

III. *The* FELLOW CRAFT's *Song,*
By brother CHARLES DE LA FAY, Esq;

I.

HAIL *masonry!* thou *craft* divine!
Glory of earth! from heaven reveal'd!
Which doth with *jewels* precious shine,
From all but *masons* eyes conceal'd.

CHORUS.

Thy praises *due who can rehearse,*
In nervous prose *or flowing* verse?

As

2.

As men from brutes diſtinguiſh'd are,
A *maſon* other men excels;
For what's in knowledge choice and rare
But in his breaſt ſecurely dwells?

CHORUS.

His ſilent breaſt *and faithful* heart
Preſerve the ſecrets *of the* art.

3.

From ſcorching heat and piercing cold,
From beaſts whoſe roar the foreſt rends,
From th' aſſaults of warriors bold
The *maſons art* mankind defends.

CHORUS.

Be to this art *due honour paid,*
From which mankind receives ſuch aid.

4.

Enſigns of ſtate that feed our pride,
Diſtinctions troubleſome and vain,
By *maſons true* are laid aſide,
Arts *freeborn ſons* ſuch toys diſdain.

CHORUS.

Innobled by the name *they bear,*
Diſtinguiſh'd by the badge *they wear.*

5.

Sweet *fellowſhip* from envy free,
Friendly converſe of *brotherhood*
The *lodge's* laſting *cement* be,
Which has for ages firmly ſtood.

CHORUS.

CHORUS.

A lodge *thus built for ages past*
Has lasted, and shall ever last.

6.

Then in our *songs* be justice done
To those who have inrich'd the *art*,
From ADAM to great BEAUFORT down,
And let each brother bear a part.

CHORUS.

Let noble masons *healths go round,*
Their praise in lofty lodge *resound.*

To the deputy Grand Master and Grand Wardens.

IV. *The* enter'd 'PRENTICE's *Song*,

By brother MATTHEW BIRKHEAD, deceased.

To be sung after grave business is over.

COME let us prepare,
We brothers that are,
Assembled on merry occasion;
Let's drink, laugh and sing,
Our wine has a spring,
Here's an health to an *accepted mason*.

All charged.

The world is in pain
Our secrets to gain,
And still let them wonder and gaze on;
Till they're shewn the light,
They'll ne're know the right
Word or sign of an *accepted mason*.

'Tis *this* and 'tis *that*,
They cannot tell *what*,
Why ſo many great men of the nation,
Should aprons put on
To make themſelves one,
With a *free* and an *accepted maſon.*

Great kings, dukes and lords
Have laid by their ſwords,
Our myſt'ry to put a good grace on,
And ne're been aſham'd
To hear themſelves nam'd
With a *free* and an *accepted maſon.*

Antiquity's pride
We have on our ſide,
And it maketh men juſt in their ſtation;
There's nought but what's good
To be underſtood
By a *free* and an *accepted maſon.*

We're true and ſincere
And juſt to the *fair*;
They'll truſt us on any occaſion:
No mortal can more
The ladies adore,
Than a *free* and an *accepted maſon.*

Then join hand in hand,
By each brother firm ſtand,
Let's be merry and put a bright face on:
What mortal can boaſt
So noble a toaſt,
As a *free* and an *accepted maſon?*

CHORUS.

CHORUS.

No mortal can boaſt
So noble a toaſt,
As a free *and an* accepted maſon.
Thrice repeated in due form.
To all the *fraternity* round the *globe*.

V. *The deputy* GRAND MASTER's *Song*.

N.B. *Every two* laſt lines *of each verſe is the* Chorus.

ON, on, my dear *brethren*, purſue your great *lecture*,
And refine on the rules of old *architecture*:
High honour to *maſons* the *craft* daily brings,
To thoſe brothers of *princes* and fellows of *kings*.

We drove the rude *Vandals* and *Goths* off the Stage
Reviving the *art* of Augustus' fam'd age;
And *Veſpaſian* deſtroy'd the *vaſt temple* in vain,
Since ſo many now riſe in great *Beaufort*'s mild reign.

The noble *five orders* compos'd with ſuch art,
Will amaze the fixt eye, and engage the whole heart:
Proportion's ſweet harmony gracing the whole,
Gives our *work*, like the glorious *creation*, a ſoul.

Then *maſter* and *brethren*, preſerve your great name
This *lodge* ſo majeſtick will purchaſe you fame;
Rever'd it ſhall ſtand till *all nature* expire,
And it's glories ne'er fade till the *world* is on fire.

See, ſee, behold here, what rewards all our toil,
Inſpires our genius and bids labour ſmile:

To our *noble grand master* let a bumper be crown'd,
To *all masons* a bumper, so let it go round.

Again, my lov'd *brethren*, again let it pass,
Our ancient firm *union* cements with the glass;
And all the contention 'mongst *masons* shall be,
Who better can work, or who better agree.

VI. *The* Grand Warden's Song. By Bro. *Oates.*

LET *masonry* be now my theme,
Thro'out the globe to spread its fame,
And eternize each worthy brother's name.
Your praise shall to the skies resound,
In lasting happiness abound,
And with sweet *union* all your noble deeds be crown'd. { Repeat this line.

CHORUS.

Sing then, my muse, to mason's *glory,*
Your names are so rever'd in story,
That all th' admiring world do now adore ye!

Let harmony divine inspire
Your souls with love and gen'rous fire,
To copy well wise SOLOMON your *sire.*
Knowledge sublime shall fill each heart,
The rules of *g'ometry* t' impart,
While *wisdom, strength* and *beauty* crown the glorious *art.* { Repeat this line.

Chorus. *Sing then, my Muse,* &c.

All

All charged.

Let noble BEAUFORT's health go round,
In ſwelling cups all cares be drown'd,
And hearts united 'mongſt the *craft* be found.
May everlaſting ſcenes of joy,
His peaceful hours of bliſs employ,
Which time's all-conquering hand ſhall ne'er, ſhall ne'er deſtroy, { Repeat this line.

Chorus. *Sing then, my muſe,* &c.

My Brethren, thus all cares reſign,
Your hearts let glow with thoughts divine,
And veneration ſhew to SOLOMON's *ſhrine.*
Our annual tribute thus we'll pay
That late poſterity ſhall ſay,
We've crown'd with joy this glorious, *happy, happy day,* } All Sing.

CHORUS.

Sing then, my muſe, *to* maſons *glory,*
Your names are ſo rever'd in ſtory,
That all the admiring world do now adore ye.
To all the *noble* LORDS that have been *grandmaſters.*

✱✱✱✱✱✱✱✱✱✱✱✱✱✱✱✱✱✱✱✱✱✱✱✱✱

VII. *The* Treaſurer's *Song.*

N. B. The two laſt lines of each verſe is a *Chorus.*

GRANT me, kind heaven, what I requeſt,
In *maſonry* let me be bleſt,
Direct me to that happy place
Where *friendſhip* ſmiles in every face ;

Where

Where *freedom* and ſweet *innocence*
Enlarge the mind and chear the ſenſe.

Where ſcepter'd *reaſon* from her throne
Surveys the *lodge*, and makes us one;
And *harmony*'s delightful ſway
For ever ſheds ambroſial day;
Where we bleſt *Eden*'s pleaſure taſte,
Whilſt balmy joys are our repaſt.

No *prying eye* can view us here,
No *fool* or *knave* diſturb our chear;
Our well-form'd *laws* ſet mankind free,
And give relief to *miſery*:
The *poor* oppreſs'd with woe and grief,
Gain from our bounteous hands *relief*.

Our *lodge* the ſocial *virtues* grace,
And *wiſdom*'s rules we fondly trace;
Whole *nature*, open to our view,
Points out the paths we ſhould purſue.
Let us ſubſiſt in laſting peace,
And may our happineſs increaſe.

To all *charitable* maſons.

✻✻✻✻✻✻✻✻✻✻✻✻✻✻✻✻✻✻✻✻✻

VIII. *The* Sword-bearer's *Song*.

N. B. The laſt two lines of each verſe is the Chorus.

TO all who *maſonry* deſpiſe
This counſel I beſtow:
Don't ridicule, if you are wiſe,
A *ſecret* you don't know.

Your-

Yourſelves you banter, but not it,
You ſhew your *ſpleen*, but not your *wit.*
With a Fa, la, la, la, la.
Inſpiring *virtue* by our rules,
And in ourſelves ſecure,
We have compaſſion for thoſe fools,
Who think our *acts* impure:
We know from *ignorance* proceeds
Such mean opinion of our *deeds.*
With a Fa, &c.
If *union* and *ſincerity*
Have a pretence to pleaſe,
We *brothers* of *free-maſonry*
Lay juſtly claim to theſe.
To *ſtate-diſputes* we ne'er give birth,
Our motto *friendſhip* is, and *mirth.*
With a Fa, &c.
Then let us laugh, ſince we've impos'd
On thoſe who make a pother,
And cry, the *ſecret* is diſclos'd
By ſome falſe-hearted brother:
The *mighty ſecret*'s gain'd, they boaſt,
From *poſt-boy* and from *flying-poſt.*
With a Fa,-la, la, la, la.
To all *maſters* and *wardens* of regular *lodges.*

IX. *An* ODE to the *Free-maſons.*

N. B. The two laſt lines of each verſe is the *Chorus.*

BY *maſons art* th' aſpiring domes
In ſtately *columns* ſhall ariſe:
All climates are their native homes,
Their learned actions reach the ſkies.

Heroes and *kings* revere their name,
While *poets* ſing their laſting fame.

Great, *noble*, *gen'rous*, *good* and *brave*,
Are titles they moſt juſtly claim;
Their *deeds* ſhall live beyond the grave,
Which thoſe unborn ſhall loud proclaim.
Time ſhall their glorious acts enrol,
While love and friendſhip charm the ſoul.

To the laſting *honour* of *free maſons.*

X. *An* Ode *to* Maſonry, *by brother* J. BANCKS.

N. B. The two *laſt lines* of each verſe is the *Chorus.*

GENIUS of *maſonry* deſcend,
In myſtick numbers while we ſing;
Enlarge our ſouls, the *craft* defend,
And hither all thy influence bring.
With ſocial thoughts our boſoms fill,
And give thy turn to every will.

While yet *Batavia*'s wealthy *pow'rs*
Neglect thy beauties to explore;
And winding *Seine*, adorn'd with tow'rs,
Laments thee wand'ring from his ſhore;
Here ſpread thy wings, and glad theſe iſles,
Where *arts* reſide, and *freedom* ſmiles.

Behold the *lodge* riſe into view,
The work of *induſtry* and *art*;
'Tis grand, and regular, and true,
For ſo is each good *maſon's* heart.
Friendſhip cements it from the ground,
And *ſecrecy* ſhall fence it round.

A

A ſtately *dome* o'erlooks our *eaſt*,
Like orient *Phœbus* in the morn;
And *two tall pillars* in the *weſt*
At once ſupport us and adorn.
Upholden thus the *ſtructure* ſtands,
Untouch'd by ſacrilegious hands.

For *concord* form'd, our ſouls agree,
Nor fate this *union* ſhall deſtroy:
Our toils and ſports alike are free,
And all is harmony and joy.
So SALEM's *temple* roſe by rule,
Without the noiſe of noxious tool.

As when AMPHION tun'd his ſong,
Ev'n rugged rocks the muſic knew;
Smooth'd into form, they glide along,
And to a THEBES the *deſart* grew:
So at the ſound of HIRAM's *voice*
We riſe, we join, and we rejoice.

Then may our vows to *virtue* move,
To *virtue* own'd in all her parts:
Come *candour*, *innocence* and *love*,
Come and poſſeſs our faithful hearts:
Mercy, who feeds the hungry *poor*,
And *ſilence*, guardian of the door.

And thou ASTRÆA (tho' from earth,
When men on men began to prey,
Thou fled'ſt to claim celeſtial birth)
Down from *Olympus* wing thy way;
And mindful of thy ancient ſeat.
Be preſent ſtill where *maſons* meet.

Immortal ſcience too be near,
(We own thy empire o'er the mind)
Dreſs'd in thy radiant robes appear,
With all thy beauties train behind;
Invention young and blooming there,
Here *geometry* with *rule* and *ſquare*.

In *Egypt's fabrick* * learning dwelt,
And *Roman* breaſts could virtue hide:
But *vulcan*'s rage the building felt,
And BRUTUS, laſt of *Romans*, dy'd:
Since when, diſpers'd the *ſiſters* rove,
Or fill paternal thrones above.

But loſt to half of human race,
With us the *virtues* ſhall revive;
And driv'n no more from place to place,
Here *ſcience* ſhall be kept alive:
And manly *taſte*, the child of *ſenſe*,
Shall baniſh vice and dulneſs hence.

United thus, and for theſe ends,
Let *ſcorn* deride, and *envy* rail;
From age to age the *craft* deſcends,
And what we build ſhall never fail·
Nor ſhall the world *our works ſurvey*;
But every brother *keep the key*!

---

* The *Ptolemæan* library.

A TRANSLATION of the Latin, *in the description of the banquetting hall of the lodge at* Marseilles; *for the benefit of such of my readers as are unacquainted with that tongue.*

The MASONS at *Marseilles* have erected this monument of their affection to their most beloved king.

Fidelity to God, our king and country.

Prudence.	Charity.
Fortitude.	Fidelity.
Pardon.	Filial debt.
Patience.	Paternal love.
Humility.	Obedience.
Friendship.	Alms-giving.
Piety.	Hospitality.

Here virtue, wisdom, beauty fixed their seat,
Love joins their hearts, and piety the tie.
Here peace we give, and here by turns receive,
One equal law of high and low the lot.

The master, vice-master, and whole body of the masons of *Marseilles* have erected these different examples of the virtues and monuments of fraternal liberality, proposed to the imitation of their brethren; to the honour of the supreme architect of the whole world; in the year of light 5765.

www.ingramcontent.com/pod-product-compliance
Lightning Source LLC
Chambersburg PA
CBHW030344270326
41926CB00009B/955